Be a Happier Parent with NLP

D0281496

Dedicated to Sue Knight who started me on my NLP journey.

Teach Yourself®

Be a Happier Parent with NLP

Judy Bartkowiak

For order enquiries: please contact Bookpoint Ltd,
130 Milton Park, Abingdon, Oxon OX14 4SB.
Telephone: +44 (0) 1235 827720. Fax: +44 (0) 1235 400454.
Lines are open 09.00–17.00, Monday to Saturday, with a 24-hour
message answering service. Details about our titles and how to
order are available at www.teachyourself.com

Long renowned as the authoritative source for self-guided
learning – with more than 50 million copies sold worldwide –
the **Teach Yourself** series includes over 500 titles in the fields of
languages, crafts, hobbies, business, computing and education.

British Library Cataloguing in Publication Data: a catalogue record
for this title is available from the British Library.

First published in UK 2011 by Hodder Education, part of
Hachette UK, 338 Euston Road, London NW1 3BH.

This edition published 2011.

The **Teach Yourself** name is a registered trade mark of
Hodder Headline.

Copyright © 2011 Judy Bartkowiak

Typeset by MPS Limited, a Macmillan Company.

Printed in Great Britain for Hodder Education, an Hachette UK
Company, 338 Euston Road, London NW1 3BH, by CPI Cox &
Wyman, Reading, Berkshire RG1 8EX.

The publisher has used its best endeavours to ensure that the URLs
for external websites referred to in this book are correct and active
at the time of going to press. However, the publisher and the author
have no responsibility for the websites and can make no guarantee
that a site will remain live or that the content will remain relevant,
decent or appropriate.

Hachette UK's policy is to use papers that are natural, renewable
and recyclable products and made from wood grown in sustainable
forests. The logging and manufacturing processes are expected to
conform to the environmental regulations of the country of origin.

Impression number   10 9 8 7 6 5 4 3 2 1
Year   2015 2014 2013 2012 2011

Acknowledgments

Thanks to my parents, Audrey and Dennis, who have been and still are models of excellence of all the qualities I value and want to model for my own children: love, unbridled joy, compassion, respect, resourcefulness, curiosity, friendship and downright silliness. I would specifically exclude my dad's long and rambling golf stories with very daft punch lines! I won't be modelling *them*, although I might model the tenacity with which he persists in telling them, despite the groans to stop.

Thanks to my husband and children, who appear prominently in the book, though will be amazed that I've produced anything. As far as they can see, I live in the kitchen and I don't work.

Most thanks to my dog, Roxy, who knows perfectly well what I get up to all day! Whether walking for inspiration or warming my feet under the desk, she gives me unconditional love and support.

Contents

Meet the author   ix
Only got a minute?   x
Before you begin   xii

Part one: Basic NLP principles

1 Introduction to NLP   3
    What is NLP?   5
    The ground rules   10
    Modelling   15
    Why NLP is great for your children   18

2 Identity   24
    Who am I?   25
    What do I want?   33
    Questionnaire   40
    What does it all mean?   45

3 Communicating   55
    Achieving the desired response   56
    Developing rapport   58
    Negotiating skills   63
    Giving and receiving support   66
    Embracing change   70

4 Time management   77
    Valuing your time   79
    Prioritizing   82
    Coping with guilt   84
    'Me time'   86
    Delegating   89

Part two: Applying NLP at home

5 Lack of confidence   95
    Coping with feelings of failure   96
    Not being a 'good mother'   103
    Embarrassment   106
    Envy   109
    Knowing your strengths   112
    Coping with criticism   114
    Giving your child confidence   117

	Supporting schoolwork	120
	Friends	126
6	**Guilty feelings**	**130**
	Not enough time with the children	131
	Children not eating well	133
	Coping with fear and anxiety	136
7	**Coping with change**	**140**
	Going back to work	140
	Not going back to work	143
	Becoming a stay-at-home dad	146
	And then there were two	148
	Moving house	152
	Changing schools	156
	Divorce/separation/illness/death	159
	Death of a pet	162
8	**Coping with conflict**	**166**
	Sibling rivalry	166
	Bullying	170
	Disobedience	174
	Jealousy and anger	178
	Internal conflicts	180
	Pester power	184
9	**Teenagers**	**188**
	Communicating with your teenager	188
	Teaching children to be streetwise	196
	Sexual issues	199
	Glossary	203
	Taking it further	205
	Index	206

Meet the author

I have worked with children for many, many years as a mother, nursery school teacher and a market researcher conducting focus groups and interviews with mums and children.

Children are fantastic, they are like sponges soaking up new experiences and knowledge, and they so want to please us and earn our love and approval. We are their role models, so when we look at their behaviour we see ourselves, warts and all! It was only when I discovered NLP that I realized that any change we want for our children has to start with us as parents, and it is with that premise that I have written this book.

The changes I have made using NLP over the last five years have made a huge difference, not only to how I connect with my four children, who range in age from nine to 21 years, but more importantly to my own state of happiness. It has been a real eye-opener how by simply rephrasing a question or a comment I can get a positive outcome. My friends frequently remark on my optimistic nature and I have NLP to thank for this.

I sincerely hope you enjoy the book and share what you learn with your partner and your children. *You* are the key to a whole new way of thinking and being for your family. Turn the key and find the happy parent in you.

Judy Bartkowiak

Only got a minute?

Neuro Linguistic Programming (NLP) is a coaching therapy that has long been applied in the business world and is now making an impact in education and sport. NLP teaches us new ways of looking at and managing how we:

▶ communicate
▶ deal with conflict
▶ negotiate a 'win-win' situation
▶ become solution focused rather than problem focused
▶ reframe situations
▶ access our skills and resources
▶ cope with loss and grief
▶ manage change.

NLP developed from Satir's Family Therapy and continues to develop alongside other therapies you may be familiar with such as Cognitive Behavioural Therapy (CBT) and Transactional Analysis (TA), both used extensively with children and families in counselling environments.

'Neuro' is what we think; 'Linguistic' is what we communicate verbally and non-verbally; and 'Programming' is how we process the communications and experiences we have. There is a set of ground rules which gives us a reassuring foundation for all our transactions within the family and outside.

1 There is no failure, only feedback.
2 We have all the resources we need.
3 Look for the good intention.
4 If someone else can do it, you can do it.
5 The map is not the territory.
6 What you focus on is what you get.

Our children model us naturally from birth, so how can we use this instinctive process to effect the changes we want in our family life? We learn to model individual skills to enhance those we already have and add these to our skill set.

NLP is ideal for working with children to develop their confidence, internal referencing and communication skills. You can show your children how to use these tools in their everyday life to be happier and ease their passage through life.

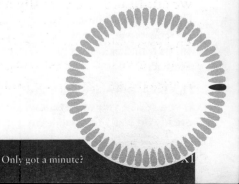

Before you begin

It doesn't matter if you've never heard of NLP – this book will explain all you need to know and give you lots of examples of how a little knowledge can go a long way. Just knowing the pillars of NLP will introduce you to a new way of parenting. There are 'Insights', case studies and tips throughout the book that will show you how NLP can be applied to everyday parenting whatever your child's age.

Part one of the book not only covers the general principles behind NLP, but also includes a questionnaire that you can use to determine how you and your child communicate and think. You need to know this in order to apply the techniques that are related in the subsequent chapters. Part two explores in more detail the practical applications of NLP in parenting.

Most chapters contain practical exercises clearly separated from the main text in boxes. These are not optional. It is by engaging with the book and getting involved that you will change how you parent and get a different, more harmonious result. Even when exercises appear to be repeated, do them again because they are slightly different according to the situation they address.

You will notice that the emphasis is on mothers and this is deliberate. While fathers play an equally important role, NLP is particularly effective in changing the negative emotions that women experience more than men, namely, lack of confidence, guilt and fear of conflict. Share the book with your partner and use it as an opportunity to agree a new parenting approach working more closely together, harnessing each other's strengths.

This book has avoided using jargon as much as possible. Where there are repeated terms and phrases that apply specifically to NLP, these can be found in a short glossary at the back of the book for quick reference.

This book will make you a stronger, more effective parent because as you read it you will acknowledge and appreciate what you already do well. You will learn to recognize patterns of behaviour and communication, observe and welcome feedback and make the changes that will bring about a new confidence in your parenting.

As you do this you will be modelling the skills of rapport, confidence, resourcefulness and resilience for your children and passing them on so that they will develop into the happy young people you want them to be.

Part one
Basic NLP principles

1

Introduction to NLP

In this chapter you will learn:
- *the basic ground rules of NLP*
- *the origins of NLP in other therapies*
- *how NLP draws on other therapies*
- *why NLP is perfect for parenting*

Neuro Linguistic Programming or NLP, as it is more frequently called, is a coaching tool that has long been applied successfully in the world of business. Companies regularly bring in NLP coaches to develop and enhance leadership and rapport-building skills, manage change, build self-esteem and establish compelling visions for employees. NLP also has a valuable role to play in organizations for negotiating and conflict management, especially at vulnerable times such as when there will be redundancies.

Surely these are the *very* skills we need as parents? More importantly, aren't these the skills we want to pass on to our children?

We should be our children's models of excellence. From when they are tiny babies they learn from us and throughout their childhood we are their role models. The NLP tools we acquire will enable us to become models of excellence for the skills we want to pass on to them so they can be better equipped for the world they live in when we are not by their side to support and protect them.

The ability to discipline and inspire, encourage, build confidence and support learning is surely a valuable parental tool. Rapport-building skills enable us to communicate well with those around us as well as with our children. There certainly will be change in our lives that we will need to manage for ourselves and our family. Being a parent can be challenging at times and the ability to negotiate with our children and manage conflict is essential. Probably the most important aspect of parenthood though, is the ability to present compelling visions of the future for our children and to demonstrate good self-esteem.

You may wonder how a single coaching therapy can have so many applications across such a wide age range. The reason is that the tools are extremely simple, which means they can be easily learned, remembered and applied to any situation and can be easily explained, even to very young children.

NLP comprises a set of ground rules or 'pillars', a number of tools and an overarching concept of **modelling** excellence. All of these can be applied just as well to a parenting application as to a business.

We all know what a tough job it is being a mum, dad or main carer of a child you love. NLP provides us with some great concepts for managing our family relationships and specifically the relationship with our children. It shows us how to allow the best in us to act as a model for them, and how to discover and harness their own strengths in challenging situations as they go through life.

You can't change your children's behaviour without changing your own. Have you heard this expression?

> If you always do what you've always done, you will always get what you've always got.

Patterns of behaviour become habits and until we are truly tested by parenthood we don't realize how these patterns are not helpful. Interactions with adults in personal relationships and at work may have been less than satisfactory, but not enough to challenge our established way of communicating. It is when we feel we are failing at the very basic and most emotionally charged relationship of all, with our child, that we stop to think and question whether we need to change our own behaviour if we want to achieve a different result.

Use this book to do something different and get a different result – the one you want. NLP gives you the tools to make the changes in your behaviour and communication that will make the difference to what you can be and achieve as a parent.

We are born with the physical ability to produce children and the resources to bring them up to be happy and fulfilled. There are times, however, when we wonder where those resources are!

Whether you are a parent, grandparent or carer, teacher, nurse or other health professional, children are an important part of our lives. We each have gifts to pass on to them and they have gifts to share with us. Children are not the enemy to be quashed and controlled, taught and moulded; they are the pioneers of tomorrow.

One of the guiding principles of NLP is that *everything* is possible and that we can achieve whatever we focus on by drawing on our own skills – because we already have all the resources we need. We can also draw on the resources of those around us. NLP assumes we can change what we do and how we think to get a different result.

Fundamental to NLP is 'modelling' and this will be covered extensively in this chapter. What it means is:

> If someone else can do something, then you can too.

You can be whatever you want to be if you copy or 'model' the quality or skill you need where you see it demonstrated in someone else. This also means that you are a model for others who want something you have that is attractive to them. Your children are born wanting your approval, wanting to model you and this book will show you how to make the most of this.

What is NLP?

Let's take a look at how NLP developed from its origins through to the latest developments in NLP thinking and how it is used today in schools and with children all over the world.

ORIGINS

Richard Bandler and John Grinder developed NLP in the USA during the 1970s. They were inspired by Virginia Satir, a key figure in the development of family therapy in the 1950s and 1960s.

Satir was the first therapist to identify the idea that a problem itself is not the problem, but the way in which we cope with it. This remains a core tenet of NLP.

Another influential therapist was Franz Perls who founded Gestalt Theory. Perls talked about aiming for excellence to reach our goals. This formed the basis of the modelling process for which NLP is best known.

He famously said, 'What is, is', and recommended us to become aware of what we are doing, how we are doing it, and how we can change ourselves, and at the same time, to learn to accept and value ourselves in the moment.

Gestalt brings the concept of 'frame of reference' to NLP: we are what we bring to parenting from our past experience, the beliefs we hold, and things we have been told that limit our self-esteem or ability to achieve our goals. We can choose to let these limit us or not. Choice is fundamental to NLP, and we each have the power of choice. Choice gives us the power we need to reject old, long-held beliefs.

The third main influence on NLP was Milton Erickson. His biggest contribution to NLP was his work on language patterns in the area of communication and rapport. He is also responsible for the idea that we *already have* the resources we need and that all behaviour has a positive intention. Erickson emphasized the need to understand the other person's 'map of the world' and acknowledge that any conflict was a result of poor rapport.

Today NLP is used in teaching, medicine, business and of course in the home within families. It is a bundle of complementary ideas that promise positive change for you and your children.

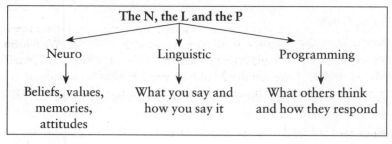

Figure 1.1 NLP.

The first column (beliefs, values, memories, attitudes) is *what* you are thinking – 'Neuro' – and this is determined by your identity, your memories and upbringing, beliefs about yourself and your values and attitudes.

The second column is what you say – 'Linguistic' – the type of words you choose and the patterns you use. That is, *how* you express yourself verbally, whether you use images, sounds or feeling words and how you limit yourself by words such as 'can't' and 'should' and so on.

The third column is the *effect* of what you say and how you say it, which become behaviour patterns – 'Programming' – that may or may not successfully get the result you want.

HOW NLP COMPARES WITH OTHER THERAPIES

Transactional Analysis (TA)

NLP is similar to TA in that they both place emphasis on how we communicate; the 'transactions' we have with one another. They assume we have a choice and can switch to another more resourceful style or mode to get a different and more positive response. How often do we say something and then realize we have not really communicated what we meant? We may have added a sarcastic element or sounded rather childish or maybe been overly authoritative. Here's a brief explanation of TA. There are some useful references in Taking it further (p. 205) if you wish to read more on the subject.

TA was developed by Dr Eric Berne. He suggested that we each comprise three parts, or states of being: Parent, Adult and Child (PAC).

Note: When talking about these *states*, we use a capital letter to differentiate between the actual parent, adult and child in question.

The Parent has a further two parts, sometimes critical and sometimes nurturing. For example, our child has an accident and cries. We swoop down and comfort him, saying, 'There there, let me have a look, shall we put a little plaster on that? Now do you see what I mean about picking up your toys? If you had done that you wouldn't have fallen over and hurt yourself.'

Here we see first the nurturing parent and then the critical parent.

It's not just real parents who have a Parent inside them, everyone does. It is the part that controls us and reminds us to behave. Even small children have this 'inner parent' and you can often see them in adult type poses, hands on hips or wagging a finger at some miscreant in the playground. There is nothing wrong with being in Parent mode, but being aware of it may help you choose whether that is the most effective mode for the situation at hand.

Then there is the Child part who wants to be loved, have fun, laugh and cry with very little sense of self-discipline. The Child in us wants to be nurtured and loved unconditionally. Children, of course, have this part along with their own Parent and Adult states, and so do we, although sometimes we need to (in NLP terms) enter our child's territory and play with them to remember what it feels like to be a child.

When you find it hard to say no, then this is your Child who wants to be loved and gain approval. Your Adult would say, 'I'd love to help but on this occasion I can't, sorry.' When you ask a question or try to find out information, this is your Adult wanting to listen and learn.

> **Tip**
> When you don't get the response you want from your child, think about which mode you used and reword the request in the Adult style, adding a sense of curiosity. For example, 'I'm wondering why you did that when you know we are in a rush,' rather than using 'Don't...' which is the Parent mode.

So that is how the communication principles of NLP link in with TA. How we *process* the communication has more in common with Jungian philosophy.

Jung

Carl Jung explains that in daily life we use thinking, feeling and sensing skills and have preferred styles of each – that is, some people are more intuitive, others more cerebral, others some sensitive and so on. You may have heard of the Myers-Briggs Type Indicator tests that some human resources departments use in recruitment, management training and employee reviews. Some of the 'types' are based on Jungian theories.

The 'Thinker' is good at analysing and interpreting data or communication but they are less adept at putting themselves in another person's shoes and being aware of the feelings of the situation. This is similar to the **'mind the gap'** idea of NLP where we learn to not react too quickly and emotionally to an input but to disassociate ourselves and think more rationally about whether it is reasonable. Drawing on the TA section earlier, this is rather like letting the Adult take over from the Child.

The 'Feeler' is good at associating with the experience, feeling what the other person is saying and feeling the same emotions. Feelers are very good at empathizing and, as a result, make very good friends and colleagues.

The 'Intuitor' has the ability to take on board details while at the same time seeing the bigger picture. Intuitors are good at summing up what others are saying and getting to the nub of the conversation, 'what it all means'.

Cognitive Behavioural Therapy (CBT)
The therapy most similar to NLP is CBT. They both acknowledge that how we behave is affected by how we think and what we believe about ourselves and others around us; that we need to change our way of thinking first and then we can change our behaviour.

Both CBT and NLP are based on the belief that emotional upset is the result of how we think and what we do, so if we change the way we think and our subsequent behaviour, this will resolve the distress.

As with NLP, CBT encourages us to confront our limiting self-beliefs (the things we think we cannot do), perceptions and negative behaviour patterns and to notice how they affect our ability to achieve our desired outcome.

Quite specific to CBT is the idea of keeping a diary to record how we have tested out new ways of thinking and responding. This isn't part of NLP but many NLP practitioners will recommend this as a way to facilitate change. If you are constantly recording, then you are becoming more aware of how your behaviour and communication is affecting your relationships.

Along with NLP, CBT is based on the idea that people act and feel, based on their map of the world (the map is not the territory) and aim to identify and change distorted or unhelpful ways of thinking by reframing thoughts in a more helpful and positive way.

LATEST DEVELOPMENTS
Since Bandler and Grinder, there have been new developments in the area of **'clean language'**, which has been used with children

very successfully. Essentially, it is the art of asking questions that are totally respectful of the child's map of the world, simply feeding their own words back to them without judgement. Clean language uses dreams and metaphor to explore feelings and allows the child to make their own interpretation of what they are feeling. This work has been pioneered by David Grove and then modelled by Penny Tompkins and James Lawley.

Sue Knight, in her latest edition of *NLP at Work* (Nicholas Brealey Publishing, 2009), has included a chapter on humour and refers to Frank Farrelly's work on Provocative Therapy. She reminds us that being able to laugh together is key to a harmonious relationship and is testament to the ultimate rapport possible between two people. Just laugh and feel how your muscles relax and you feel much less tense.

In India, BrainoBrain have been using NLP with thousands of children in combination with teaching them using a modern-style abacus to mentally calculate complex sums and build amazing levels of focus and concentration. They have seen pupils achieve astonishing results and their work is now spreading across the globe. The principle is that by physically moving beads whilst mentally calculating, this activity stimulates both left and right hemispheres of the brain. An analogy is that it is like the difference between picking up a chair with one hand or two.

Schools are using NLP to understand how children communicate and learn, and you may well have been sent information on visual, auditory and kinaesthetic learning styles (VAK), which will be covered in Chapter 2.

NLP is developing all the time, but it is in the area of working with children where undoubtedly we will witness the greatest developments in the next decade.

The ground rules

If you absorb these basic ground rules into your parenting, you will notice the difference immediately. They are positive and life changing because they offer you a different way of thinking about a situation.

Let's start with one that might be relevant for you at the moment.

THERE IS NO FAILURE, ONLY FEEDBACK

Yes, that's right – you cannot fail as a parent! However badly you might feel you're doing, look on your children's feedback as useful information to understand what's going on for them and what choices you have next.

Equally, this means that when your child feels a failure, they haven't failed either; they need to process your feedback or their teacher's feedback and learn from it. We usually use the sandwich approach when giving feedback. We notice and comment on a positive aspect first, then mention what needs work, then finish on a positive note.

IF YOU SPOT IT, YOU'VE GOT IT

What we observe in others is usually a reflection of something in us. That's how we recognize it. When you notice something in your child, ask yourself, how am *I* like that? Is your child modelling you? If it's behaviour you want, that's fine but if it isn't, ask yourself, what could *I* do differently?

ONE WORD WORKS WONDERS

On the whole, children process short sentences better than long ones, so they will understand your meaning better if you make it short and sweet, for example: 'Teeth,' 'Homework,' 'Door.' This is particularly so for teenagers who are inclined to zone out as soon as you speak.

Note that children don't understand sarcasm or facetious comments until they are in secondary school. Be clear and direct: tell them how it looks, sounds or feels to you.

THEY MEAN WELL

Tip

Behind every communication or behaviour there is a good intention – look for it. You may need to be imaginative, but it will be there. Whatever they say or do, they love you and want you to love them. At the very least, they want you to notice them. Look for the good intention in whatever they do. There is no bad behaviour, but there is attention-seeking behaviour.

MIND THE GAP

Children have an amazing ability to press just the right buttons to get a reaction from us because this is what they need for survival. They need a response. Ideally they'd like a positive response but if that doesn't look likely they go for the negative one because this still gets them the attention they're craving.

Some parents use the 'count to 10' rule to control their temper, and others will leave the room and calm down before addressing a challenging situation. Both these solutions work, but when your child does something or says something you don't like, there is an alternative.

Look up and imagine you are a fly on the wall. What would she make of it? This is called 'disassociating' and it enables you to separate your emotions from the situation so you can find the resource you need. Ask yourself what outcome you want and then express it without emotion.

On the basis that there is a good intention, NLP recommends looking for it and reappraising the event or situation in that light.

YOU HAVE THE RESOURCES TO DO WHATEVER YOU WANT TO DO

Do you remember your parents saying to you, 'There is no such word as 'can't'? Well, there is some truth in it. You and your children have a huge bank of skills, but first you need to identify them. Seek out where you have the skill and apply it to the situation.

The skill might be one you use at work or it may belong to that time before you were a parent, but the skill is there somewhere. It may help to find someone you think is a good example of that skill and ask them how they do it. You have the skill to copy someone else and this is very useful in parenting because it enables us to acquire other parents' skills.

IF SOMEONE ELSE CAN DO IT, YOU CAN TOO

All you have to do is identify what skill you need and who you believe to have it in abundance. Watch and learn from them and ask the right questions. You need to know their self-talk, their beliefs and values and break down all the elements of what they do so you can copy it. Then show your children how to do it!

IF YOU 'TRY', YOU WON'T SUCCEED

Just do it! As soon as you think you'll 'try' to do something, you have assumed you won't succeed. The same is true of asking your child to

'Try to eat something' or 'Try to be good'. 'Eat something' and 'Be good' imply successful outcomes.

....
Insight
My son used to forget to bring home his homework diary and I used to tell him, 'Try to remember your homework diary today, please.' Then I realized how unproductive the word 'try' was. So instead I noticed when he *did* remember it and praised him by saying, 'Well done for remembering your homework diary, you are so well organized.' He beamed back. He doesn't forget it nowadays because he has taken on the belief that he is well organized rather than the belief that he is forgetful.
....

THE MAP IS NOT THE TERRITORY

Children see their world quite differently from us; their priorities are different, their time scales, beliefs and the way they best communicate.

NLP talks about stepping into another person's shoes. Get down to your child's level, play on the floor alongside them and understand why only *that* piece of Lego can possibly go on that model they are making, or why this Barbie needs to have that shoe she's looking for, or why they can't possibly come now because they are busy playing.

LOOK FOR THE GOOD INTENTION

Children do what they do because they get what they want by doing it – your attention, usually. How can you give them that result without the behaviour? They want and need attention and love, but their means of getting it isn't always acceptable to us. What they want is our time and that isn't always easy to give. We all have busy lives and lots of demands so how can we give our children that time they want?

One way of doing this is to take a moment to explain that if they do what you ask quickly, you will have more time to play with them, read them a story, or whatever you know they want to do with you. Children of all ages love to help, and getting them to do something with you such as laying the table, finding items in the shop or tidying away their toys, is a win-win, which as we all know in business and work situations is the key to harmonious negotiations. Simply bribing them with sweets or pocket money is a not a win-win.

USE RESOURCEFUL, NOT LIMITING, LANGUAGE

Avoid words like:

▶ never
▶ always
▶ can't
▶ should
▶ must.

These words are limiting because children do not 'always' do something or 'never' do or say something. There aren't many things they 'can't' do or 'should' do, but there are lots of things that if they did them would result in a better outcome. By focusing on the desired outcome, you can reword an instruction so that it is clear and easy for them to understand and comply with.

Hence, 'You should wash your hands before eating,' becomes 'Let's wash your hands before you eat because they are dirty.' 'You can't have those sweets,' becomes 'If you eat those sweets now you won't enjoy your tea,' and 'You never say you're sorry when you are unkind,' becomes 'I like it when you say you're sorry because I know you didn't mean to be unkind.'

Assumptions about how your child feels or thinks are what NLP would describe as 'unecological'. Being ecological, in NLP terms, is about considering and respecting others and asking rather than making assumptions about their feelings. A typical example of making assumptions would be saying things like, 'I know you're thinking...' or 'I expect you will say...'.

The word '*don't*' is called an '**embedded command**' because what a child hears is whatever follows it. Have you heard the expression 'don't think about pink elephants'? First, you have to conjure up a pink elephant in order to make sense of the instruction. Children invariably do the thing we've just told them not to do because subconsciously we have just told them to do it. Change your 'don'ts' into 'dos' and tell them what you *do* want.

BE SOLUTION FOCUSED

When you feel overwhelmed, and we all feel like that sometimes with our busy lives and demands on our time, it's useful to have a solution-focused strategy.

Here's a good NLP device for doing just that. This is a great exercise to do right now before you continue reading this book.

Have a go

Imagine you are going to sleep right now with all the problems you feel you have. Amazingly though, during the night something magical happens and you wake up the next morning to find all your problems have disappeared.

What is the first thing you notice? What is happening? What has changed?

Although you have only imagined the dream, you have also imagined that the problem is solved and, by looking for the signs that things are different, you are encouraged to be solution focused so that the real situation looks very different now. You can identify what you need to do. Maybe you know what chapter to look at in the book.

Modelling

We have learned that there are many similarities between NLP and other therapies such as TA, Jung and CBT, but there are also three uniquely different principles of NLP.

Two of these relate quite specifically to how we communicate and think and these are covered in the next two chapters on identity and communicating. The third is **modelling.**

In the context of NLP, modelling is copying not only the way someone does something but understanding and absorbing their underlying beliefs about it. By modelling, you can identify a skill in someone else and observe it, ask about it and practise it until it becomes part of your own repertoire of skills.

Imagine someone is modelling out of clay and they have in their mind what they want the lump of clay to become. After a time, you too can see what they are making but you wouldn't be able to copy it without knowing what they were thinking about. It is the same with NLP modelling; not only do we need to watch carefully how someone does the thing we want to copy but we also have to ask them questions to decipher what is going on in their head. We need to understand their beliefs and values first.

Let's practise with a seemingly trivial skill like doing a cartwheel. Children do them all the time but there was a first time, wasn't there? Children watch others and for a long time they look like frogs jumping their legs round their hands. Eventually they learn that in order to succeed they have to trust that they will be upside down and balancing on one hand, albeit for a second. They can copy the action but they must also take on the belief and trust in order to successfully achieve it.

Have a go

If you don't want to do a cartwheel, how about another skill such as putting on lipstick without a mirror? Do you believe you can do it? You need to have this belief before you start. What other things can you do without a mirror and what belief do you have about doing them? Now transfer that belief to where you need it for the lipstick exercise and have a go. What else can you now do with this new belief?

What behaviours would you like to model? Be observant and note the things you admire in your friends, acquire those for yourself and then show your children how to do this. You will need to be very observant and become a bit of a detective to find out how they do what they do. Sometimes they won't know themselves and you will have to really probe their beliefs about what they do.

Insight

I watched with awe every week as Rachel, a forward in our hockey team, tackled relentlessly. I wanted that skill.

I observed her over a few matches. I then copied the way she moved faster than me, closer to the ground, running with her head down and didn't take her eyes off the ball. I copied this but it still didn't work, although I noticed some improvement.

So I asked her what she was thinking just before she decided to tackle. She said, 'I think to myself, "I am going to get that ball."' That helped but it still wasn't enough.

So I asked her about the ball. 'Why do you want that ball?' I asked her at half time. 'Because that's my ball, I want my ball back.'

I realized that this was the difference that would make the difference. My belief was that this was 'their ball' and I wanted it from them, but her belief that it was *her* ball was more powerful as a winning belief. As I went in for the tackle I kept saying to myself, 'That's my ball and I'm going to get it back.' It worked.

The great thing about modelling is that anyone can do it and when you introduce this skill to your children they can acquire the skills they want as well.

Insight

My son was having problems making friends and was going about it by annoying the other children to get attention. I asked him who he thought was good at making friends. 'Jack,' he said without hesitation.

'How does he do that?' I asked.

'He lets anyone join in his games and he's always friendly and smiley,' he replied.

I suggested that he copy Jack. When he's not sure what to do or say he could think, 'What would Jack do in this situation?'

This worked very well and he fitted in much better in the playground as a result.

Modelling is studying how people who do something 'with excellence' think, feel and behave so that we can do it too. Just imagine if you could take the best aspects of everyone you know and embody them in yourself. It isn't just about modelling people you know well, you can also model those you watch on TV, or people you have a more indirect contact with such as a colleague or client, a teacher at your child's school or another professional.

Insight

I have always admired Jenni Murray. I wanted to model her interviewing style, which I think is excellent. I listened attentively and, of course, couldn't question her. As she's a radio presenter (Woman's Hour on BBC Radio 4) I couldn't watch her either. I read articles and pieced together what made her tick. I concluded that she had unconditional curiosity, and then took on that belief for myself. As a result my body language shifted to show the curiosity I was feeling. I matched her pace changes, hesitations as she considered what to ask and her tonal inflections as she delved deeper. My interviewing style improved considerably as I (in my mind) *was* Jenni Murray.

Using these NLP modelling skills we can learn to do anything so let's look more closely at modelling.

Our children love us and from birth they watch our every move and listen to our voice. They have amazing powers to discern our voice in a crowded room even when they can't see us and many babies can distinguish their own parents' car arrive home.

They are completely tuned into us and love us unconditionally. It is this focus and attention that enables them to learn from what we do, to mimic us. From us they learn to eat, walk, talk and interact socially. We don't take advantage of this natural instinct of theirs as much as we could. In modelling, we learn how to watch and copy and understand the underlying beliefs that enable someone to do that thing that we want to do. The association between beliefs and behaviour is a differentiating feature of NLP and is demonstrated very clearly in modelling.

NLP assumes that *we* have the resources ourselves. We can do anything and all we need to do is retrieve the resource from the area of our life where we used it last and apply it to where we need it now. If we want to fine-tune that resource and can see someone else do what we want to do – but 'with excellence' – then we can model them and acquire that skill for ourselves.

Why NLP is great for your children

NLP is great for parents and children because it focuses on the positive. The tools are easy to explain even to very young children and fun to experiment with. Results are immediate and applicable to any aspect of life whether at home, in the classroom, playground or in the workplace. If one tool doesn't solve the problem then there are others that will resonate more or work better for you in that situation.

NLP is fun. We so often forget in our busy lives that our child's map of the world is different from our own. The map is not the territory; your map is huge and encompasses worlds they are totally unaware of, such as the workplace, your financial situation, relationships with friends and extended family, the political and economic environment you live in and the world you travel in. For them, the territory is smaller, more intense and they are more vulnerable because they are dependent on you for all that they need: love, support, encouragement, respect, security, food, education and other practical necessities like toys and TV!

Using NLP thinking we are invited to enter their territory and enjoy it by walking in their shoes, listening and using their language and mannerisms to understand it. By doing this, we can communicate in a way that resonates with them from a close distance emotionally, where we have good rapport. As you do this, you will capture much of their excitement and energy.

Tip

It is fun to watch some of their favourite TV programmes when they're not in the room. Pick a character from the show and copy their body language, their expressions and notice what they talk about. It can be a real eye opener! These characters are part of your child's world and are influencing them as their role models. Being aware of this and associating with them yourself is a great way to understand you child's territory.

The tools of NLP are simple to use and explain to children. They are fun to try out because children can see how they can change the meaning of the communication if they use different structures. You already have a bond with your child so there is a trusting environment to experiment with new approaches together. They know you have their best interests at heart and by introducing them to another way of communicating, whether verbally or non-verbally, this will give them options they can call on whenever that situation arises again.

Children are great at playing make-believe, so getting them to adopt new ways of saying and doing things comes as second nature. They can visualize really well and understand metaphors – one thing representing something else. Try asking your son how he is like Superman or whoever his favourite character of the moment is. Ask your daughter how she is like Hannah Montana. You could tie it in with whatever they are doing at school and ask how a Victorian child, or a character from the book they are reading, might feel.

Tip

Kerys takes ages to go to bed and finds all sorts of things she has to do before she goes upstairs. When her mum wants to speed her up, she asks how Scooby Doo goes to bed. In no time at all, Kerys is up there asking for a Scooby snack!

NLP is ecological in the sense that it respects that we all have choices. Children have the choice whether to be angry or jealous or sad about something because we can help them use an NLP tool to reframe a situation so it makes sense to them in their 'map'. It gives children a measure of control over their lives so they can learn to communicate in a way that will bring them their desired outcome. This gives children the all-important confidence they need in every area of their life. It gives them strategies for coping with people they find difficult (whether they are peers or teachers), for enhancing friendships and increasing motivation in work and sport. Children are fast learners and their patterns of behaviour are easier to change than adults whose habits are well entrenched.

Childhood should be a happy and carefree time but we all know and possibly remember that it is not always so. Children feel sad and angry, bully and get bullied in the playground, struggle with their classwork and exams, experience peer-group pressure and have to deal with bereavement and changes at home that are beyond their control. Surely the best skill we can pass on to them is self-esteem, belief in themselves and their abilities, and the skills to achieve whatever they want in life?

If you learn the NLP tools and understand the concepts, you can explain them to your children. More importantly, they will give you the confidence and self-esteem to parent your children in a positive way avoiding conflict and stress.

Here are some very basic first NLP tools to work through with your child. Imagine the ground rules mentioned earlier are the backdrop and this next set of exercises is the prologue introducing the main players or actors. You keep the ground rules in your mind, while playing with NLP with your children to show them how what they think affects what happens. You can even use these tools with very young children.

1 ANCHORING A GOOD STATE

You know how your mood can really affect your day?

> **Insight**
>
> If I am late setting off on the school run, hit all the traffic and then can't find anywhere to park at school, I get stressed and irritable at the slightest thing for some time afterwards. I notice how my whole body is in that tense state. I apply the brakes a bit sharper than normal, take corners a bit faster and my reactions are jerky and stiff rather than relaxed and fluid. The muscles in my arms feel tight on the steering wheel and my back is more upright and stiff as a rod as I glare at the traffic holding me up.
>
> When I notice this I put on the radio and sing along to the music. My state instantly changes and I feel relaxed and happy again.

So how can you change state? How when your child is in a state that is unhelpful, can you help them change it?

The first time, do it together with your child so they can see what they need to do. This exercise will be referred to several times throughout the book.

Anchoring exercise

Think of a happy time for you, maybe a holiday or an outing with your partner, a funny programme on TV or a night out with a girlfriend. Relive the moment you've chosen and remember how you felt, what you saw, what you heard and what a good feeling it was. When the memory is at its height and you're smiling or chuckling away as you recall it, do something physical to 'anchor' it for you, such as squeezing your earlobe or tapping the steering wheel. The next time you feel yourself getting stressed again, repeat this physical '**anchoring**' action to remind yourself of that relaxed and happy state. Physical cues work for kinaesthetic learners but visual learners could use an image, and those who are auditory learners could hum a tune or imagine listening to a piece of music as their anchor.

Anchoring exercise for children

Ask them to think about a fun time, something they really enjoyed, a party or maybe a movie. Show them how to anchor it and make sure they do it a few times to reinforce it.

Children do tend to get themselves into a state and having the ability to change state is a very useful tool. When your child is really happy and pleased with life or proud of an achievement, ask them to squeeze their ear lobe and capture the moment. Tell them that if they do that every time they are feeling on top of the world, then when they are feeling sad they can repeat that physical action and it will remind them what it's like to feel good about themselves again.

2 BEING IN RAPPORT

Rapport is how we get on with people, make connections and form friendships. Some people are naturally good at this. Ask your child who they think are the popular children in their class. What makes them popular? It is possible to watch these people and learn how they do it. Here is a basic exercise in developing rapport.

3 ACCESSING RESOURCES

Children very easily notice someone who can do something they can't
do, whether that be a handstand or scoring goals, looking pretty or
getting top marks. They don't so easily notice what *they themselves*
do well and although modern parents are quick to praise their child,
unless your child believes in their own abilities, the praise is quite
empty and meaningless.

Be specific when you notice what they do well so that they recognize
it as a skill that they can apply in other situations.

Metaphors work really well to get children talking about themselves.
Ask your son or daughter how they are like a pizza or how they are
like their favourite singer, football player or TV character. These

comparisons focus on the positive and help them identify their strengths.

Where there is a gap between how they want to be and how they think they are, talk about how this person they admire does what he or she does. Watch them and observe what they do and how they seem to do it. Find out about them: do they hold a certain belief about themselves that enables them to perform in a certain way?

If their hero is closer to home, a relative or friend maybe, then it is even easier to copy the behaviour and find out what has inspired it, the thought processes and beliefs.

This is in a sense an extension of the matching exercise but at a distance, unless the model can be encouraged to help in a direct way.

Children are very receptive to these games and enjoy them. It requires you to interact with them in a very direct way, which shows love and support. Observe when they use a new pattern of communication and try some out yourself as well.

As you continue through this book you will find lots of examples of how you can share the lessons with your child. I'm sure you will agree with me that NLP is a fantastic gift for children.

2

Identity

In this chapter you will learn:
- *about NLP logical levels*
- *how you communicate*
- *how you think using NLP meta programmes*
- *how to embrace change*

There are so many changes we take on board when we become a parent for the first time and along with the physical exhaustion of parenthood and accompanying challenges to our confidence, is it any wonder that we stop and think 'who am I now?'

Before children, we knew who we were and probably only had to think about ourselves. We could have spent hours discussing our thoughts and feelings about every issue with friends at work, in the pub, over meals and so on. Having had children, time constraints mean we don't have that luxury these days, but do take some time to read through this section and re-establish who you are, and think about your beliefs and values, skills and resources. You will certainly impress yourself and stand a few centimetres taller as a result.

Friends are great at restoring our confidence, aren't they? What would we do without them? Remember though that we, as mums and dads, don't believe all we are told and we have selective hearing. How much easier to take a criticism than a compliment! When someone you love and trust tells you they think you've handled a situation really well, what do you do? Do you shrug it off as just your friend being kind and supportive? Or do you take it in, reflect on what you did and learn from it? Maybe not. You were given some positive feedback and didn't make good use of it. We all do that, but once you've read this book you will make better use of feedback and be better at giving feedback that others, particularly your children, can learn from.

Who am I?

If you don't know who you are then how can you consider change? Change from what to what? Let's take a moment to explore *you*.

First, let's separate roles from identity. You probably have many roles as a parent, such as peacemaker, teacher, disciplinarian, playmate and comforter. In your workplace, you have other roles associated with the work you do. Among your friends and family, other roles are required and you may have different roles in each relationship you have. This is not your identity. These are 'hats', to use a metaphor, which you can put on when called upon to do so. You can switch hats when you need to but your identity will stay the same.

This chapter is about questioning who you are and what you stand for – your identity – which is the totality of your beliefs and values. If this book is to be successful, you need to look at changing how you do things, so first you need to establish firmly who you are.

So, what makes you who you are?

LOGICAL LEVELS

NLP's **logical levels** help us understand how each aspect of our life plays a part in establishing our identity.

Figure 2.1 *The six logical levels.*

- ▶ Your *environment* is where you live, your own cultural background, where you work, your personal circumstances, and how they affect you.
- ▶ Your *behaviour* is what you do in that environment, the things you do on a daily basis such as your work, looking after your children and your home.
- ▶ Your *skills* are how you do these things, the resources you have and what you have learned to do.
- ▶ *Beliefs* are what you hold to be true about your skills, behaviour and environment. Beliefs change as you age and experience new things. Your *values* are what guide and form you as a person; the rules you live your life by. They tend not to change.
- ▶ *Identity* is the sum total of all these – environment, behaviour, skills, beliefs and values – and defines you as a person.
- ▶ Your *purpose* or vision is what you want to achieve in life.

Your cultural background brings with it certain beliefs and values about how a parent should behave, how your children should be brought up and what is expected of you as a parent. Your own parents will have been role models who, while you may accept or reject their beliefs and values, you will still be influenced by. Sometimes we resist against how we were brought up and want to do things completely differently, just because we can. It may be because our environment really *is* different or that we only *perceive* it to be through the media or experience.

Penny's mother didn't work; she lived for her children and cooked for them every day, helped them with their homework and was always at home when they got back from school. She had given up a good job when she had children because her cultural background dictated that she would not be a working mother.

Penny herself worked her way up to an interesting and well-paid job before she fell pregnant with her first child. Her mother assumed she would give up work as she did, or at least work part-time, but Penny wanted to keep her independence and carry on working. She enjoyed her job and the people in her team. It took a while to find someone she liked and trusted for childcare and, although there was quite a bit of juggling, she did manage to carry on working and even got a promotion.

On the face of it, she had succeeded in what she wanted to do and her husband was very supportive. However, Penny felt a failure. She cried when she missed her son's first steps and when she had to go to work when he was unwell. Her mother did not comment, but between them was a sense that Penny was a disappointment as a mother. She felt guilty and tired and whenever her son misbehaved she blamed herself for being a 'bad mother'. Her beliefs and values were compromised and every day she felt torn between what she thought she should do based on how she was brought up and what she wanted to do for her own fulfilment. She believed herself to be selfish in 'wanting it all'.

We all have expectations based on our childhood and on what is happening around us, and these can be at odds with the norms of our own generation. This can be even more extreme if our family is from a more traditional background with rigid rules about what women should do as mothers, and what men should do as fathers. Different religious backgrounds also influence our environment and can be confusing and restrictive compared to that of our peers.

Think about your environment. How does it affect you and what you can do, the choices you make and the expectations people have of you? What about what you watch on TV, the celebrity mums we hear about, the magazines we read. There are a great many reality shows on TV, wife swap programmes and programmes about children's and family issues. How have these left you feeling about a mother's role today?

As a single mother, step-parent, stay-at-home dad, grandparent or main carer, beliefs about these roles have changed significantly since we were children. How has that affected you?

Beliefs determine who you are; they make you the unique, wonderful person that you are and the mother or father that you will be. They are what you hold to be true about yourself, those around you, your environment and the world in general.

Values are what you are guided by, how you live your life, what you believe to be right or wrong. You know what a value is when someone does something you feel strongly about and react to emotionally.

While people generally change their beliefs about things based on new experiences, people they meet, places they visit and cultures they learn about, *values* tend to remain with you and are things you will cling to and possibly even fight for. For example, as children we *believed* in Father Christmas, didn't we?

When you use words like 'can' and 'can't', these words reflect your beliefs about yourself and others.

Words like 'should' and 'shouldn't', 'good' and 'bad' reflect your values and what you feel to be important. 'A parent should keep their children safe' is your value. 'It is bad to steal' is another value.

We live by our values and beliefs and pass them on to our children. It is important to know what they are and to question them. Sometimes we inherit beliefs and values from our parents that are no longer appropriate in today's society. Maybe you can think of beliefs you held before you had children that you have now had to rethink.

Your current environment and your childhood together form your beliefs and values. It might be helpful to note down here what you feel is expected of you based on how you were brought up. Here are a few starters:

Mothers should:

A good mother is someone who:

What I loved most about my mother was that she:

I admire mothers who:

I wish more mothers would:

I get cross when I see mothers:

The best mothers:

I would be a better mother if I:

.... is a good mother because she:

Has this given you some ideas about your values and beliefs about good mothers?

Now, separate the beliefs from the values. The *beliefs* are views and opinions that you hold and you can imagine that these might change as circumstances change for you. The *values* are those statements that are what makes you who you are and under no circumstances would you change them.

Other ways in which we learn what is perceived to be 'good' and 'bad' come from feedback at school and from our peers as we are growing up. Our cultural background may dictate one set of 'rules', but we then set that alongside what we see around us and consider acceptable based on feedback from others.

One of the problems we can experience with our beliefs is when they limit us. If you were brought up to believe, as Penny was, that good mothers don't work, this belief is limiting you – how can you be 'a good mother' who works, and maintain these beliefs?

Instead of being limited by your beliefs, let them go! Look at them in a positive light and see where that takes you. Start by thinking about what you're good at. Use the list below to record all your qualities and the things that you do well in every part of your life, work, home, friends, sport and so on. On the right hand side complete the sentences as shown. For example: I am good at driving so my belief about myself is that I am careful, conscious of other people (drivers) around me, abide by rules (of the road) and have good concentration.

I am good at .... My belief about myself is that I am:

I am good at .... My belief about myself is that I am:

I am good at .... My belief about myself is that I am:

I am good at .... My belief about myself is that I am:

I am good at .... My belief about myself is that I am:

Now what does that mean in the context of you as a parent? How can you apply these positive beliefs about yourself to parenthood?

Remember to include your role at work. Even if you just have a part-time or voluntary job, help out at the local parent and toddler group, you will be using skills and qualities that reflect your beliefs and values. If you have a demanding work role and spend less time in parent mode, you still need to think about what skills and strengths you bring to your parenting role from the workplace.

SKILLS

CASE STUDY

Sue worked in HR and frequently gave presentations at work and trained many of the senior managers on people skills, communication and negotiating. She had to stand in front of people more senior than herself and train them. She set them exercises and gave them feedback and everyone commented on what a great job she did. But at the end of each day she returned home to put Jacob to bed and she just could not do it without losing her temper. Jacob ran all over the house, he threw his pyjamas in the bath, he refused to brush his teeth and he was just 'downright naughty' according to Sue. Sue's partner would return from work to find her in tears over the bedtime battles.

I asked Sue to list the qualities and skills she used at work, to write down what she did well and what she believed about herself. She wrote:

▶ I know how to get people's attention in a room
▶ I can get people to listen
▶ I am a good speaker
▶ I explain things well
▶ I can get them to take part in the exercises, even the silly ones

▶ I get them on my side

▶ I can get them to laugh with me.

At that point she looked up and smiled. 'I am a good communicator and I can get people to do what I want them to do. So why can't I get Jacob to bed?'

The trouble was that the beliefs she had about her skills in the workplace had not transferred home. She had not communicated effectively with Jacob. So we talked about how she achieved what she did at work and very soon she realized that with a lower tone of voice, good eye contact, humour and clear instructions she would be able to get Jacob to bed. And of course she did!

Beliefs can limit us because they are self-fulfilling. If we believe something about ourselves, that can become our truth. How often do we hear people say, 'I can't stand up in front of people', 'I can't stand heights', or 'I'm scared of dogs'? Sometimes we hide behind those beliefs rather than challenge ourselves for fear of failure, and as a result we don't give ourselves the opportunity to succeed.

At the top end of the logical levels we have *purpose*, your vision or goal in life. Do you have a sense of purpose?

Have a go

To help understand your purpose in life, try writing your own obituary.

How would you like to be remembered?

_____

_____

_____

What would be written on your tombstone?

_____

_____

_____

It's gruesome, I know, but a good insight into what you want to achieve in life and what you want your children to be left with when you are gone.

Insight

I have a friend who regularly tells me 'I can't decide what to do'. The NLP response to this is, 'What if you *could* decide what to do, what would it look, sound or feel like?' Once she has answered this question, her belief is no longer limited – she has, in effect, already decided. She could then choose whether she wanted to commit to what it entailed.

It's the same with all sorts of beliefs. Try playing for a bit.

Have a go

Go to a mirror, but don't look into it yet. Think yourself into believing that you are beautiful – absolutely drop-dead gorgeous. Now look in the mirror. What do you see? Yes, a fabulous-looking you. Now repeat the exercise thinking yourself really ugly and look again. Yes, not such a great look is it?

You see, what you believe about yourself, good or bad, comes true.

You can turn this technique to your advantage by *believing* that you are a good mum or dad. If you need ammunition, write a list of all the reasons why you're a fantastic parent.

I'm a great parent because I:

1

2

3

4

5

See how you can harness your beliefs and make them work to your advantage.

Since the start of this chapter, we have explored your identity, your beliefs and values. It may have been a while since you did this. Take the opportunity now to think about what beliefs have changed for you.

I used to believe:

Now I believe:

I used to believe:

Now I believe:

I used to believe:

Now I believe:

Your values may be unchanged, but have you ever written down what they are? Are they the same as your partner's? How are you passing on your values to your children? Are you a good example of your values for them to model?

Sometimes, because of your environment or your personal situation, it can be hard to live according to your values. It can feel uncomfortable to be in this sort of imbalance, so how are you finding opportunities to live out your values?

Your identity has changed as a result of becoming a parent. How has that changed who you are?

I used to think I was:

Now I know I am:

What do I want?

I have already mentioned the idea of a desired outcome or compelling vision. This is an important concept in NLP, and therefore you need to have one. So often, as parents, we muddle through the day as best we can, hoping to get everything done and avoid any disasters.

This is what NLP calls 'away-from' goals. This means we are aiming away from disaster rather than 'towards' anything. With away-from goals, it is hard to feel good about yourself because you are looking for the *absence* of something – not easy. Here's an example of my away-from day:

- I get up and try to find something to put in my son's lunchbox that he will like.
- I try to get him to eat something nutritious and filling for breakfast.
- I try to get him out of the door and into the car without forgetting anything he needs for school.
- I hope that the traffic won't be too bad so we won't be late.
- I get home and walk the dog.
- I try not to forget to walk fast because I need to lose some weight.
- I try to get down to some work and hope I don't get distracted by emails from friends or by checking Facebook.
- I collect my son and try not to be late.
- When we come home I try to get him to do his homework without making a fuss.
- I make him some supper before bed.
- I try to get him to bed, even though he wants to stay up with us.
- I try to spend 'adult time' with my partner because I don't want us to grow apart.

Have a go

1 Go back through that bullet list and underline all the away-from thinking.
2 Note how many times the word 'try' is used. If you only try, you won't succeed because the word 'try' assumes you won't actually do it.
3 Note all the negatives and the negative assumptions that imply failure.
4 How would someone living like that feel they ever had a good day?

The goal needs to be within your control. It's no good having a goal that requires other people to fulfil it because you can't control them. Many of us would probably like to wave a magic wand and have

34

our children impeccably well behaved, do as they are told, be kind to their siblings and respectful of us. This will only come about by changes you make, so your goal has to be for *you* – something you can control and monitor, measure and reward.

If you can't measure your successes daily then you can't enjoy your desired outcome. Decide on how you will know if you have achieved your goal for the day or the week. What will you notice that will indicate success? What will be different?

You may have to be quite specific about the measure. Vague goals like 'I will be more patient with my toddler' or 'I will spend longer helping my son with his reading' are not *measurable*. For example, decide exactly what time you will spend helping, and what strategy you will put in place to keep your patience with your toddler.

In CBT, therapists recommend keeping a diary. This is a great way of monitoring your goals and ensuring you record how well you are doing.

HOW MUCH DO YOU WANT IT?

Your desired outcome will only be achieved if it's really what you want. Half-hearted or well-intentioned goals tend to fall by the wayside very quickly, especially if they are simply goals that someone else has suggested or goals you think you ought to have, such as New Year's resolutions!

The next few exercises will help you decide which goals are truly compelling visions.

Finding your compelling vision

First, write down what you want in your own words. I expect there are several things you want, not just one, so write them all down and we can work with them all. (You don't have to think of ten things.)

I want to:

1 _____

2 _____

3 _____

(Contd)

4 _____

5 _____

6 _____

7 _____

8 _____

9 _____

10 _____

Now let's work on them together. As you already know, NLP is a positive force so we need to make sure your wants are phrased in the positive, rather than things you want to stop doing or being. Now write them out again as *positive* aims.

1 _____

2 _____

3 _____

4 _____

5 _____

6 _____

7 _____

8 _____

9 _____

10 _____

Now looking at these positive statements and desires, combine some of them into sentences that describe what you want. Your compelling vision will work best if it encapsulates all the elements in a way that is quite specific and not too general. It needs to be achievable and you need to set a timeframe rather than set it vaguely in the future.

As covered earlier in the book, you know that you already have the resources to be this person you want to be. You can and will achieve your vision, and by drawing on skills and qualities you have in other parts of your life, you can bring them into your parenting by acknowledging their existence and feeling good about yourself. At the moment, you may not feel so good about yourself, but let's examine your strengths and skills so you can match them to what you need in order to achieve your goals.

Take each of your positive statements (from the exercise above) and think about where you have demonstrated it in some other part of your life. If you have said, for example, that you want to be patient with your children, think about where and in what other circumstances you are patient, such as waiting for a delivery, a train, or exam results. How have you done that? What strategies have you used?

NLP, like many other therapies, makes good use of time lines in a number of ways, and setting desired outcomes or compelling visions is a good use of them. It facilitates working with future time and reflecting on past times; bringing skills from the past through to the present and on into the future.

Time line exercise

Pick a room or space that will allow you to mentally draw a line on the floor. Stand on the line at where you judge today to be if the line represents your life from past to future. You don't need to be specific about where the line starts and where it ends – it does not have to be birth and death! Some people find there is a natural starting point for them and a natural end point. It could relate to your marriage or partnership, before you had children, or when you left home, or it could relate to the emotional journey you are making in self-development. So find your spot that is 'today' and stand on it.

Now look forward towards the future and think about where the point is that represents the time when things will be 'better' or 'easier' for you as a parent.

Go and stand there and think deeply about what this point means for you.

If you are a visual sort of person, what do you see around you in this imaginary place when things are different? How do you look and what do others see when they look at you and your family?

(Contd)

If you are more auditory in your approach, what do you hear, what sounds are in your head? What do others hear? What would you say about yourself and your family at this point?

If you tend towards the kinaesthetic, how are you feeling? How comfortable do you feel in your skin – are you warm or cold? How are others around you feeling? What do you sense?

When you are satisfied that you are really experiencing what this better place might hold for you, squeeze your earlobe. This is called anchoring (see p. 20). You can repeat this physical action whenever you want to remind yourself of what you're aiming for. Do this a few times to establish the anchor.

What is different now? Can you pinpoint what has changed and what is the difference that *makes* the difference? What has happened between the point representing today and this future point you are standing at? Looking back along the line towards today's point, can you see stages at all? Can you see individual moments or steps in the journey?

Now walk back towards today's point, thinking about what those stages are and decide which is the first one. Step on it and think about this first change, how you are going to make it and what needs to happen. Do this for each stage until you arrive at the point representing the place you anchored and anchor it again.

We have talked about the idea of a compelling vision, a desirable outcome that is positive and achievable with the resources you already have. Remember that you have the resource of learning from others who have some skill you need. Along the way to that vision there are steps that you need to take to make the changes that will bring you closer to that vision. As you make the changes, use your anchor to remind you of what you're working towards.

This all sounds very positive but you may have a mischievous negative voice inside your head telling you that you can't do it. This is called a 'limiting belief'. Someone or several people who had significant influence in your past may have told you that you couldn't achieve or succeed, that you were in some way not good enough. If only this didn't happen! But just as it is done to us, it is possible to do it to our own children without thinking, especially if we don't understand their territory and assume it's the same as ours. Argue with the negative voice and question it:

'and what if I *could*?'

Follow this with other phrases that focus on achieving your goals such as:

- ▶ 'What would it look like?'
- ▶ 'What would it sound like?'
- ▶ 'What would it feel like?'

By asking ourselves these questions we associate with our goals. This means that we acknowledge not only that they *can* happen, but that they *will*, because they can only happen if we can visualize them. If we can imagine it happening then it will happen.

Insight

My husband is a great cyclist. Cycling is his passion. It really matters to him to cycle up steep hills. Me, well my cycling goals are away-from, so I don't manage them. I look at the hill and say 'I can't get up that.' Then I tell myself off and say 'I will cycle up as far as I can and then walk.' That of course is a ridiculous goal and you won't be surprised to know that I walk up most of them. The goal that would get me up the hill on the bike rather than pushing it up would be to say to myself, 'I *will* cycle up that hill. I can already see myself at the top feeling very proud and looking forward to the downhill afterwards!'

Focus on the feelings, vision and sounds of achieving your end goal and take each step along the way as a triumph as the goal gets closer and easier to imagine.

Some people find it easier to travel with a close friend or with their partner on this parenting journey. It makes sense to work together, helping each other to make the changes that will make the difference, and celebrate the victories along the way with someone who knows what it has taken to make them.

Knowing what you want and working towards it, is not a one-off event in life. Once you have applied these lessons you will need to reapply them as your child gets older and the challenges change.

Go back and look at the statement you made earlier about your desired outcome. You may now want to reword it in the light of your exercise with the time line. Do that and then write it down somewhere where you will see it daily.

My vision is to:

It will look like:

It will sound like:

It will feel like:

Questionnaire

How we think and the way in which we filter our communication is called our meta programme. I have included just some of these key meta programmes in the questionnaire.

The idea behind completing this is that, having looked at your logical levels and set your goals, you will be better able to work through the following more situation-based chapters if you know how you think, communicate and process information.

When I refer to specific NLP terms such as visual, auditory and kinaesthetic learning, you will then know which you are and can apply the learning more appropriately.

In each question there are three options and more than one of them may be true for you. Tick the one that is *most true* for you in each case.

VISUAL/AUDITORY/KINAESTHETIC

1 You get a phone call from a good friend. Do you:
   a picture the person who is phoning you?
   b enjoy hearing his or her voice?
   c feel happy that they have called you?
2 Your child is not feeling well. Do you:
   a look anxiously at them?

    b tell them they'll soon feel better?

    c worry about them and give them hugs?

3 When you have lost something, do you:

    a look up and to the left trying to picture where you had it last?

    b talk to yourself about where it could be?

    c hunt around everywhere?

4 Would you like your children to:

    a look to you for advice?

    b listen to your advice?

    c follow your advice?

5 How do you prefer to get the news?

    a Newspaper

    b Radio

    c Internet

6 How particular are you about your appearance?

    a I would not be seen dead looking less than my best

    b I like it when someone remarks about what I'm wearing

    c I like to feel comfortable

7 Which words are you most likely to use?

    a See, look, watch

    b Listen, hear, tell

    c Feel, touch, do

8 Which of these phrases sound most like you when you get cross?

    a Just look what you've done

    b I've told you before

    c I feel really angry

9 If you feel uncomfortable somewhere is it likely to be because:

    a the place is ugly and unattractive?

    b it is too noisy or too quiet?

    c it is too hot or too cold?

10 When your child does something funny do you notice:

    a their face or expression?

    b what they said?

    c how you felt?

If you've mostly ticked 'a' then you are *visual*. If you've mostly ticked 'b' then you are *auditory*. If you've mostly ticked 'c' then you are *kinaesthetic*.

You may well find that you and your child do not neatly fall into any one category but will use all three at different times. They will still have a preferred way of processing and you can check out which they prefer by asking, 'Would you prefer me to tell you, show you or do it with you?'

Circle what you and those important to you are so you have it to hand:

I am	visual / auditory / kinaesthetic.
My child .... is	visual / auditory / kinaesthetic.
My child .... is	visual / auditory / kinaesthetic.
My partner is	visual / auditory / kinaesthetic.

AWAY FROM/TOWARDS

Have you noticed whether you work *towards* things or you go through life trying to *avoid* things? Do you aim for good health or want to avoid being ill? Do you save for something or do you put money away for a rainy day?

1 When you are able to save money do you:
    a save for something specific such as a holiday or Christmas?
    b save for a rainy day, emergencies, or just in case?
2 Do you try to be healthy because:
    a you want to live a long and active life?
    b you don't want to be ill?
3 Thinking about your job:
    a do you want to earn loads of money and have an interesting job?
    b is it better than nothing?
4 Do you want your children:
    a to be happy and successful?
    b to not fail in life?
5 Thinking about your appearance do you want to:
    a look great?
    b not look like a dog's dinner!?

If you've mostly ticked 'a' then you have a towards preference; if you mostly ticked 'b', your tendency is away-from. There may be some areas where you tend to be 'away from' because of past experience. For example, if you have been made redundant recently, even a usually towards thinking person might become away-from when they are looking for another job.

I am	away from / towards.
My child .... is	away from / towards.
My child .... is	away from / towards.
My partner is	away from / towards.

CHOICES/PROCESSES

Some people love to have **choices** or options rather than have everything planned out and organized for them. Having choices is important but it can also hold you back from moving forwards because you are so embroiled in the choices that you never make a decision.

1 When you are planning a holiday do you:
   a spend ages considering all the possibilities?
   b decide on somewhere quite quickly and book it?
2 Thinking about your career do you:
   a research all the possible jobs and compare them?
   b apply for a number of jobs, decide which and then go for it?
3 Before you go out to a party do you:
   a spend ages deciding what to wear?
   b just pick something and wear it?
4 When cooking a meal do you:
   a enjoy looking through recipes?
   b have a rough meal plan for the week and stick to it?
5 Christmas is a time for you that is:
   a full of decisions about what to get for the children.
   b about making lists which you follow.

If you ticked mostly 'a' then you like choices; if you ticked mostly 'b' then you tend to prefer **processes** and plans without options along the way.

I prefer	choices / process.
My child .... prefers	choices / process.
My child .... prefers	choices / process.
My partner prefers	choices / process.

BIG-CHUNK/SMALL-CHUNK

This is the difference between wanting the big picture and being happier with details. Big picture or **'big-chunk'** people are great at having ideas but not so good at seeing them through, as their organizational skills and eye for detail are less developed.

1 Thinking of your career do you have:
   a a vision of where you're going?
   b a very specific idea with specific steps along the way?
2 When you use a recipe do you:
   a follow it roughly but adapt it to suit?
   b make sure you have all the ingredients and follow the recipe exactly?
3 When someone gives you some information do you:
   a follow it roughly, getting the general idea?
   b follow it precisely and make notes?
4 When you're weaning your baby do you:
   a follow the guidelines but do your own thing?
   b follow a precise guide to the letter?
5 Do you use a shopping list?
   a Just for the essentials but mostly get ideas as I shop
   b I have and follow a list for everything

If you have ticked mostly 'a' then you are big-chunk; if you have ticked mostly 'b', you are likely to be **small-chunk**. It is not better to be one or the other. Some tasks require big-chunk thinking and some really need small-chunk. My husband hates it when I accuse him of being small-chunk when I simply mean that he is missing the bigger picture – but I'm the one who needs a sat nav for Christmas because I set off with only a vague idea of where I'm going!

I am	big-chunk / small-chunk.
My child .... is	big-chunk / small-chunk.
My child .... is	big-chunk / small-chunk.
My partner is	big-chunk / small-chunk.

ASSOCIATE/DISASSOCIATE

1 When a friend tells you they are worried about something, you:
   a feel it as if it were happening to you
   b listen and offer support
2 During weepy films, you are:
   a the first one to cry, you have your tissues ready
   b amazed at everyone around you crying, it's only a film

3 How involved do you get in your child's life outside the home?
   a I know all their friends by name and what's happening in their life
   b Not much, so long as they tell me where they are going
4 When someone describes their holiday to you, do you:
   a really imagine you are there?
   b lose interest after a while?
5 If you and your partner or a friend have a disagreement do you:
   a get very upset about it?
   b soon forget it because it wasn't important?

If you've mostly chosen 'a' then you tend to associate with people and situations, so you probably establish rapport very quickly. If you scored mostly 'b', you disassociate and tend to be less involved emotionally in relationships.

I tend to   associate / disassociate.
My child .... tends to   associate / disassociate.
My child .... tends to   associate / disassociate.
My partner tends to   associate / disassociate.

There are a number of thinking patterns that we use in addition to those mentioned. I have only included the main ones but you can find the whole list and detailed explanations in Sue Knight's *NLP at Work* (see Taking it further).

What does it all mean?

So now you know how you prefer or tend to communicate and how you process communication and thoughts, but what does it all mean and how can you use this knowledge?

By understanding someone else's map of the world, you will make an even better connection and build rapport. Here are some of the ways people with different processing systems view the world. If you want to connect with them you need to match your way of speaking to their way of processing. If you have a child who thinks one way, and you feel they would benefit from using a different filter, then here are some ways to use the information with them.

You know which preferences you have from the questionnaire on pp. 40–45. The information below will help you make the best use of your preference and that of your child and partner.

VISUAL/AUDITORY/KINAESTHETIC (VAK)

Taking VAK first, you will now know if you are mainly a Visual, Auditory or Kinaesthetic learner. Have you worked out what your partner is and your children?

Visual learners
If you are visual, you tend to think in pictures and images even to the extent that when someone is telling you something, you are visualizing what they have said. You prefer to see information written down so you prefer emails and texts rather than phone calls. You notice people's facial expressions and how they look, what they are wearing and will be the first to notice they have a new hairstyle. You are observant and will spot whether your child looks tired or sad, happy or worried about something without needing to ask.

Trust your judgement because your eyes are your great asset and you have a finely-honed talent for using them. Be aware, however, that others who are not visual will not see things the way you do and you may be hurt by their lack of observation. Appearance is important to you but someone less visual will not notice it. They are not being unkind; they simply function differently. You need to ensure that you listen to what people *say* rather than just take in what you can see, and consciously tune in to atmosphere rather than observe the surroundings – listening and feeling may be less natural for you.

How do you recognize if your child is visual? They will show you things rather than tell you. They will place a great deal of importance on how they look, what their room looks like and how you look. They will observe your facial expressions and not need to be told you are angry or upset but will, at quite an early age, recognize this for themselves.

> **Insight**
> In our Montessori school I noticed that children responded differently to the learning materials. Some focused on the sound a letter made and enjoyed making the sound, sometimes quite loudly! Others kept stroking the sandpaper letters and enjoying the feel of the shape. Others loved to write the letter again and again, getting pleasure from its appearance. The Montessori teachers worked with their natural preferences and achieved great results.

Auditory learners

If you are auditory, you tend to notice what is said to you and pay attention to what you yourself say. You notice noises and like music; you may be quite musical and play an instrument. Hearing what others say is important to you, so noisy rooms or poor acoustics will bother you. You want to say things rather than show someone, and you want others to listen and remember what you've said. If they are not auditory they may disappoint you; for them the written word may come more naturally. You enjoy the radio and getting information aurally rather than reading, and you enjoy phone calls rather than text messages.

Insight

My brother is an auditory person and loves to discuss, ask questions, and talk about anything and everything. He is great at parties and he's very popular. However, his emails and texts are short to the point of rudeness. He uses a bare minimum of words, sometimes just one 'yes' or 'OK' and you're left wondering what you asked him in the last email!

Because he is auditory, he latches onto words used incorrectly or lazily and takes everything you say quite literally. He remembers exactly what question was asked and all the points made.

You may not be surprised to learn that he is an excellent lawyer!

An auditory child will respond better to being told rather than being shown and will have a good memory for what they are told.

Kinaesthetic learners

If you are kinaesthetic, this means you are conscious of atmosphere, temperature and you are more aware than most of physical contact and feelings. You are sporty or enjoy doing things rather than being sedentary; you are an active person. Connecting physically with your friends and family is important for you because actions count for more than words. You probably touch friends as you speak to them, getting in close. Emails and texts are not as satisfying as actually meeting up with people, which you do as often as you can.

A kinaesthetic child will also be active and affectionate but they may not realize their own strength so they could be a bit rough and resort to bullying if they can't make themselves understood with words. They will enjoy sport and being active and enjoy physical activities. Sitting still in a classroom will be quite difficult and they will need outside play time to keep them from fidgeting and getting bored.

Tip

Knowing what learning style you prefer may help explain why you feel as you do and why you find it easier to connect with some people and not others. If their preference is different, they may not be 'speaking your language'. Use the ideas from this chapter to help you connect at a deeper level.

TOWARDS/AWAY FROM

To succeed in life we need positive goals rather than negative ones, so if you now realize that you tend to operate on an 'away from' basis, then this is a bit of a wake-up call to reframe or relook at how you live your life and introduce some positive thinking both for you and your child. If you are 'away from' you will pass this on to your children – they will be doing their homework to *avoid* getting into trouble rather than because it will reinforce what they've learned at school. They will eat what you give them to *avoid* you getting cross rather than because they want to eat healthy food.

If they get into this sort of pattern it will be harder for them to be self-motivated to succeed because they are putting their energy into not failing. You and they need positive goals for where they want to be in life rather than trying to avoid where they don't want to be. To turn this self-talk into the positive, challenge them when they say 'I don't want to...' and ask them what they *do* want. If they say 'I can't', say 'And what if you could?' Follow this up by getting them to visualize what the possibilities are.

Away-from children may avoid commitment to friendships for fear of rejection and they will avoid asking questions in class for fear of looking silly or getting it wrong. You can encourage them to be towards by rewarding them for taking small steps to overcome this habit and show them by your own actions how they can become more towards by taking some risks yourself.

Some people focus on what they want, have a positive goal and go for it. An example of this might be a child who wants another child's toy and goes to grab it. This is a towards action. You would be towards if you think in terms of what you want to be doing in five years' time, how you want your home to look, the education you want for your child and so on. Another child may want to avoid bad results or conflict, so their behaviour would be risk averse. They may be more anxious to avoid confrontations and play safe. They may be rather shy. If you are away-from, your actions are based on avoiding problems or conflict, so you may be more cautious.

Jessica is away-from. She doesn't like people to be sad or angry, she doesn't like arguments or raised voices and doesn't want people to not like her. She works hard but does so to avoid trouble at school, and she has lots of friends to avoid being on her own. She doesn't like sport much because she doesn't want to look silly or sweaty.

Lucy is towards. She works hard at school so she can get good marks, get a good job, earn lots of money and go travelling. She is ambitious and packs her life full of all the things she wants to do – netball, tennis, seeing friends and catching up on her favourite TV programmes. When she plays sport she wants to win.

CHOICES/PROCESSES

'Process' people can seem rather inflexible to a 'choices' person as they like to stick to a plan or list and get on with it without being distracted by choices. But then again, choices people can be stuck in another way and become so overwhelmed with possibilities that they can find it hard to choose between them, making decisions and commitments hard to make.

Children can also be choices or process people and you know which your child prefers. Sometimes even though your child enjoys choices, you have to make a decision. Offer your child a reduced number of options, either of which is acceptable to you, and remove those that aren't. For example, he may not want to get dressed, so instead you can offer him a choice of whether to wear this or that, to get dressed in his room or the bathroom.

We use all these preferences at one time or another. Who has not deliberated about whether to buy a lipstick in this colour or that one? That said, we do still tend to have a prevailing style – choice or process. Some of you will really enjoy that choosing process and others just want to get it over and done with and get on with the next purchase. A matching eyeliner, perhaps?

By knowing where your preference lies and those of your partner and children, you are well placed to communicate with them in a way that they can easily respond to without having to 'translate' or be confused.

Some people like to have choices. They enjoy the idea of considering all their options and often discussing them, but don't want a decision from you – they just want to have the choice. Others prefer more process-based decision-making and have plans and strategies with few choices because choices confuse the situation.

My brother first researches all the holiday options, decides and then lists everywhere he wants to go and makes a daily plan. He likes to travel on his own to avoid other people's choices and he has a ticking off the list process.

My dad, however, loves choices and lingers over many a glass of wine with my mum, painting literary pictures of all the countries they've been to and want to visit again. They read travel articles, talk to friends, collect brochures and take out their photo albums to remind themselves of places they've been to over their 60 years of travelling. Choices take up a lot of their chatting time and they love it. They do eventually book something, but for them the emphasis is on the choices rather than the plan.

The answer is to use this information to understand those you live with, those you work with and those with whom you need to communicate. It is not a matter of one being better than the other, but awareness of your pattern will help you recognize when you need to be more process driven if you have to make a decision, and when you can afford the luxury of time spent considering choices. If your partner is one and you are the other that makes for a good balance because you can help each other. You can imagine if you were both choices people, no one would ever make a decision!

Tip

Focus on your desired outcome for the situation or communication, and phrase what you say to fit the other person's map of the world.

BIG-CHUNK/SMALL-CHUNK

It helps to know which preference you and the person you are communicating with, have. Detail really matters to some children – they will draw in detail, talk in detail and attend to detail in the way they dress, behave and speak. Others will be more broad brush-strokes and just give you an outline. Notice what your child is and by matching it, you will speak the same language, whereas if you provide detail where they want the outline, their attention will wander while trying to pick out the main drift which may have got lost in the detail.

Lots of parents talk to their child at length explaining in detail why they must do something, but if the child is big-chunk, this will be a waste of time. Equally, a small-chunk child will want the detail and not just be told to do something without knowing the full story.

If you like detail, you may be a scientist, accountant or someone who enjoys figures and facts and likes them to be correct. Every aspect of a problem will be addressed, and you will enjoy tables comparing products or details on the back of packets in the supermarket. You feel cheated if you just have vague facts and want to know the whole story. Sometimes though it is important to see the big picture and a combination of skills is of course ideal. If your partner is one and you are the other this is a 'belt and braces' relationship with one of you generating the ideas and the other fleshing it out and taking responsibility for the detail.

Lauren and Bill are married and work together. He is big-chunk and has some great and quite scary business ideas, most of which have been successful, but only because Lauren makes him sit down and work out the figures first. She formulates the plan and lists exactly what needs to be done, she researches options and together they decide on each step. He tends to get bored and frustrated with the detail but knows that the combination of both their strengths will result in the best outcomes.

Children are like that too. Some like lots of information and can quote you facts about dinosaurs or their video games, and all the cheats and the scores on each Pokémon card. But others have a better concept of the game itself, its overall aim and how to play it. If your child likes detail they will want to know the rules of games and want to stick to them; they will like facts and figures, will probably be good at maths and enjoy the process of working out the right answer. They may be better at spelling than writing stories because they're less confident with thinking creatively and want to know exactly *what* to write.

....

Insight

My husband, Edward, is small-chunk. He likes to read instructions even if he knows pretty well how to do something and he reads and follows recipes and timings to the second. Detail is very important and he reads articles in full in newspapers, never speed-reads and has an excellent memory for facts. He doesn't have big ideas, but is very good at seeing through other people's

(Contd)

ideas and ensuring every detail has been considered. I am big-chunk and have no patience for detail. I just want a rough idea of what needs to be done and hand him the instructions if there's a problem. I rarely follow recipes in detail and prefer just to throw things together with a rough idea of what will result. You can imagine who the better cook is!

ASSOCIATE/DISASSOCIATE

The experience of truly being in your own body and hearing what is being said to you, seeing the person's face and responding with feeling to what they are saying is to 'associate'. It can also be referred to as empathizing. Young children are often excellent at this quite naturally and then lose the skills as they go to school and learn that some measure of protection is needed to avoid being hurt. The opposite, to 'disassociate', is where what is happening almost seems to be happening to someone else, as if you were a fly on the wall watching the conversation and watching your own reactions as a spectator.

It is a great asset to be able to both associate and disassociate when you need to. If a friend is sharing a confidence and needs your full support you may want to associate to give her your full attention. If, however, your boss is having a bad day and is getting on your nerves or giving you a hard time, you may want to disassociate so you don't get upset or annoyed.

Some NLP practitioners help patients suffering with phobias and post-traumatic stress syndrome by teaching them how to fully disassociate so they can learn to cope with stressful situations. Disassociation distances yourself from the emotions and allows time and a calm atmosphere to enable you to slow down and control your reactions, so that they are more reasonable and manageable.

You can teach disassociation techniques to your child as a way for them to cope with difficult situations.

Disassociation techniques

Ask your child to picture the scene as if it's a film, to name the characters, describe them and even give them pretend names. Some children like to give them funny names or even rude names or names from their favourite TV show.

They should put themselves in the film and give themselves a name (not their own, ideally). Then ask them to 'run the film' as if they are shooting it as a cameraman.

Ask them questions as they describe the scene: What is happening? What did he say? What did she do?

It sometimes helps children to disassociate and see the situation from another angle. If your child doesn't see that there could have been a different result from the one they are upset about, ask, 'What else could [your child's made up name] have done?' or 'What else could happen? Could there be a different ending to the film if someone had done something differently?'

You might find this technique useful when you have arguments with teenagers. When you disassociate you appreciate how high pitched and squeaky your voice sounds and how your face and body posture appear. Relax your shoulders and neck and take your voice down to your chest and then lower to your stomach. Slow down the pace. It will sound more authoritative and what you say will have more impact.

The following filters were not covered in the questionnaire, but are interesting to add here so you know something about them.

MATCH/MISMATCH

Do you notice how similar you are to others or how different? Do you like to be the same as others or do you like to be different? It's quite easy to spot. When someone says 'Yes, but...' they are '**mismatching**' or if they tend to disagree or point out something wrong or incorrect about what you have said, they are mismatching.

Young children often want to match – play with the same toy, collect the same cards, ask for the same Christmas present as their friends and eat what their friend eats – but as they get older they gain confidence and their own preferences emerge. Teenagers often mismatch their parents to express individuality and assert their independence.

PAST/PRESENT/FUTURE

Have you heard the term 'living in the moment'? It refers to the concept of being firmly in the present rather than dwelling on what has been or what you will do in the future.

Children live in the moment very well, whereas we, as adults, tend to be planning what we need to do later in the day or tomorrow or next week. We miss what's happening right now. We can learn from children to enjoy what we are doing now and notice what's around us, how we are feeling and what is enjoyable about this minute.

If you think a lot about the past, reflecting on how you could have handled something better, you might miss the opportunity to experience life as it happens. Similarly, thinking about the future means that you are racing through life missing what is happening now. Take a moment to be aware of *now* and how you're feeling at this point on your journey through the book and how you feel as a parent in this moment.

INTERNALLY/EXTERNALLY REFERENCED

Do you usually check with your friends before you make a decision? Do you check reviews, best buys, ask around? Some of us prefer to include the views of those around us before making a decision or expressing an opinion. Such a person might ask, 'What do you think of this…' and take on the opinion of the person they are asking (**externally referenced**). Others appear more self-confident and make decisions based on their own experiences and rarely consider the opinions of others. In parenting we tend to notice what other parents do, and behave similarly to our peer group because this is easier for us, rather than imposing different standards of behaviour. However, if you live in a mixed cultural relationship or environment you may need to be more internally referenced. Children need to learn to switch between internal and external referencing and access both simultaneously.

THE PROGRAMMES COMBINED

If you combine some of this information, you can see that an auditory small-chunker will be good at reading music, but the auditory big-chunker will just go to a piano and roughly get the tune by instinct with the sound in his head but no knowledge as to the actual notes. A visual big-chunker will draw in the outline, but the visual small-chunker will enjoy getting the detail correct. Add to that away-from and towards, and you have a child who wants to get it right (towards) while the other does not want to get it wrong (away-from). The choices child will spend ages trying to decide what to play or draw; the process child will simply get on with drawing or playing something.

Are these ways of seeing starting to take shape for you (visual), sound interesting (auditory), or feel right (kinaesthetic)?

3

Communicating

In this chapter you will learn:
- *how you communicate best*
- *how to get the response you want*
- *how to give and receive practical feedback*
- *negotiating skills*
- *how to pass these skills on to your children*

NLP is rich in ideas for improving rapport and this is what we need to communicate well.

VAK learning styles were covered in the previous chapter as were some of the meta programmes:

▶ associated/disassociated (connecting with your own feelings or standing apart and viewing them like a fly on the wall)
▶ away from/towards (avoiding something or positively aiming for something)
▶ internally/externally referenced (checking in with your own values or looking for the approval of others)
▶ big-chunk/small-chunk (big-picture or detailed thinking)
▶ choices/processes (options or plans)
▶ matching/mismatching (looking for similarities or differences)
▶ past/present/future (living in the moment).

If you become aware of these thinking patterns, you can match them to achieve better rapport with the people you are communicating with.

There are also filters we use that get in the way of clear and clean communication such as:

▶ *distortions* – assumptions about someone's thinking or behaviour, including mistaken cause and effect – the idea that

someone makes you feel something when in fact you *choose*
to feel it

▶ *deletions* – vague statements, vague comparisons (e.g. better
than, worse than)

▶ *generalizations* – words such as everyone, no one, never, always,
must, should, etc.

When someone you are communicating with uses any of these filters,
you need to challenge them to get clarity. The easiest and least
offensive way is simply to repeat what they've said with an upward
inflection at the end to imply a question and emphasize the filter. For
example, they say, 'I always use cloth nappies', you say 'You *always*
use cloth nappies?', and they may then amend the generalization to
explain that they might use disposables on holiday or when they have
a babysitter. This way you have a more interesting conversation,
information is more accurate and you achieve better rapport.

You will improve rapport by matching verbal language in terms of
pace, volume, rhythm, tone and pitch. Correctly done it will seem as
if you speak the same language and have so much in common, but do
it parrot fashion or like an actor without sensitivity or good intention
and it could be seen as mocking and insulting.

Non-verbal language – how you stand, how you hold your head,
facial expressions and your whole body posture – needs to closely
reflect the person you're talking to so that you are mirror images of
each other. This again improves rapport.

Tip
> Think of people you know who communicate well. Copy what they do and,
> if you can, find out their underlying beliefs because this will have informed
> their behaviour.

Achieving the desired response

We know what we mean and *we* know what we want to happen,
what we want the response to be, but how often do we get it right?
Also, even with the best intentions, we get tired, stressed and upset
so that our state isn't always resourceful and effective when we
communicate with our children. Let's face it – sometimes we just
say the first thing that comes into our head and then back-peddle as
we try to undo what we've said in haste. Here are some useful NLP

techniques to get ourselves into that better, more resourceful place to communicate effectively so that we do get the desired response.

Tips for achieving a desired response

▶ Ask yourself, what is their good intention?

▶ Consider what response you want to achieve.

▶ Anchor a resourceful state where you won't easily be provoked and you will feel relaxed, regardless of what your children are doing.

▶ Use your child's preferred language style: visual, auditory, or kinaesthetic. This gets you on their wavelength, in their territory, and they understand more easily what you want from them and can do it. If they are visual, a note works well.

▶ Use the Adult voice rather than the Parent to give information.

▶ Describe what you see and let them take remedial action. Words like 'should' tend not to get the desired response and instead result in resentment.

For example:

'I see you are watching TV' is better than 'You should be doing your homework, not watching TV.'

'I see you have left your uniform on the floor' is better than 'Don't leave your clothes all over the floor.'

▶ Less is more for children so avoid long sentences, lectures and stories of martyrdom. Use one word when you can; it tends to have more effect.

For example:

'Joe, shoes' is better than, 'It's no wonder I'm exhausted, picking up your shoes every day. I'll trip over them one day and break my leg and then you'll be sorry.'

'Emily, plate' rather than, 'I'm not your servant you know. You treat me like one, leaving your plate there for me to clear away.'

▶ Talk about your feelings rather than theirs.

For example:

'I don't want you to leave your shoes on when you come into the house because they could be dirty' is better than, 'You're so lazy you can't be bothered to take your shoes off when you come in and you leave dirty marks all over the carpet for me to clear up, you just don't care.'

'I feel embarrassed when you interrupt me when I'm talking to a friend' rather than, 'Sam, you are so rude, what will Jane think when you keep on interrupting me? She'll think you have no manners at all.'

So to recap, anchor a resourceful state, decide what you want to achieve and communicate it effectively. Remember the map is not the territory; they see things, hear things and feel things differently.

What are they really communicating? Put yourself in their shoes and enter their territory.

Developing rapport

Do you remember the first time you visited a foreign country and tried to communicate? You may speak a bit of schoolgirl French but you know that this is woefully inadequate when you want to ask the way to somewhere and understand the reply!

You try a phrase but it isn't quite right judging by the look on their face so you try another and the moment has gone. Their attention has moved on and you are left frantically trying to work out what they said and what it means. While we think they are speaking a foreign language, they of course are thinking just the same. So how do we communicate with them?

Sometimes we try to mime. We act out what we want and we mimic each other's gestures to show we understand and want to be friendly. In NLP terms, we call that 'matching' and it's a great way to establish rapport.

▶ The first thing to do is to make *eye contact* with them if you can. I know sometimes you may be negotiating by phone or by text message, but where possible try to do it face to face and eye to eye because not only can you gauge reactions, it is also more respectful and initiates rapport.

▶ *Mirror* your child's body posture and body language. Sit if they are sitting and mirror their position so you are on the same wavelength. This also helps you get into their shoes and see the situation from their point of view.

▶ Then *match* your child in terms of language – visual, auditory or kinaesthetic, and volume, tone and pace. This way you're both talking the same language. It's best not to match any swearing or name calling though!

▶ Try to *reflect* back to them their own words and keep sentences short. Show you understand by saying things like 'I understand you are feeling (give it a name, ideally the word they used).'

▶ Look for opportunities to *compromise* so if they want to do something that is unacceptable to you, suggest you both sit down and work out some options. This is a sort of brainstorming where you can both consider what options are available. Write them all down, their suggestions and yours, even ones that you won't accept. Then suggest which ones you can jointly cross out because they aren't acceptable to either of you. Look at the rest and for those that you won't accept, explain why.

▶ Explain in terms of how *you feel*, not simply what they should or shouldn't do, can or can't do. Put your point simply and clearly in the Adult voice rather than Parent or Child. Parent would be 'you can't'; Child would be 'you won't'. Adult voice is more reasoning and explanatory.

▶ It will help to discuss the *desired outcome* because they may only see one course of action towards a goal they've set. But if they are thinking small-chunk in detail, they may not have considered the big-chunk overall objective and this may open up more possibilities for compromise.

Matching has to be done subtly. You can imagine how ludicrous it would look if you made it really obvious. It would look as if you were making fun rather than wanting to show your love.

Use their own words and expressions without correcting them and you will enter their world. From there you can gently draw them back into yours with their willing participation. You can achieve great rapport and leadership if you can show you understand their needs.

Use the VAK knowledge you have to help build rapport. To check their preferred language patterns, ask them a simple question about something that excites them. Check that you ask the question in a way that offers them the chance to select their own language. For example, you could say, 'What was the party like?' or 'How was it at Jo's house?'

This might be the response from a visual child:

> *'There were shiny balloons like dinosaurs and there was this silly clown, he kept pulling plastic rabbits out of his trousers! Joe was sick all over Ben's back and it looked really gross, you could see everything he had for tea, even the green jelly, yuck!'*

An auditory child might respond:

'There were these great balloons like dinosaurs, one went off 'bang' right next to Jaya and she screamed so loud that the clown cried. He had those squeaky rabbits he kept pulling out of his trousers. Then Joe sicked up his tea all over Ben's back so he shouted at him and the clown laughed and hiccupped all at the same time!'

A kinaesthetic child might say:

'There were these dinosaur-shaped balloons and we kept trying to pop them by jumping on them. One popped right next to Jaya and she screamed. The clown had loads of plastic rabbits that he took out of his trousers, it was so funny. I tried to grab one. Then Joe was so sick down Ben's back, it really stank and Ben pushed him over. It was a great party.'

Can you work out how to match your child's language?

Let's say your daughter has trodden on her little sister's finger and this isn't the first time she has 'accidentally' hurt her. She is 'a blamer' (using Virginia Satir's categories) and her little sister has learned to be a 'placater'.

You	Sarah, look what you've done. Molly's finger is really red and sore. (visual)
Sarah	I didn't touch her. (kinaesthetic)
You	When will you see how unkind you're being to her?
Sarah	I hate her, she's so mean. She pinched me.
You	Look she's crying now.

Or you could use her preferred style and communicate like this:

You	Sarah, you've hurt Molly. She is upset. (kinaesthetic)
Sarah	I hate her, she's so mean.
You	You need to be more careful around her, she's smaller than you.
Sarah	She pinched me.
You	I'm sure she didn't mean to. She loves you but she's younger than you and she doesn't realize it hurts to pinch. Now give let's give her a hug and make up.

Rapport is essential in bringing up your children and communicating with them. Rapport builds trust. It relies on you identifying how your children tick. Apart from the language aspects we have spoken of, there are other aspects of rapport around how your child sees the world and how they need communication packaged.

CHUNKS

Children, just like adults, have a preference for information presented either in detail (small chunks) or in general (big chunks). If you present it the 'wrong' way it can be difficult for them to process.

Let's say you need to go shopping. With a small-chunk child you would present it like this: 'We are going to catch the bus and then go to Smiths to get your stationery for school, then to Next because I have to take a shirt back for Dad, and then we need to pop into Tesco to buy some food for tea.' If you child is big-chunk, you would say, 'We are going shopping and have a few chores to do so let's get ready shall we?'.

You will have a preference too. Do you sometimes think 'too much detail!' when someone is explaining something to you? Or do you think you need more detail if someone is telling you something more 'broad brush'? Be aware of what you prefer and notice how your child responds; perhaps you chunk differently. If your child needs detail, they will respond better if you feed them the detail they need to feel secure and, equally, if his eyes glaze over as you explain things in detail, perhaps this is just too much for him.

CHOICES

Some children need to have choices, even artificial choices, whereas others find this confusing and just want to know what's happening and when, i.e. more process than choice. It can be overwhelming for a child who prefers process to be given choices.

Matt is fairly action packed and just gets on with life, taking it at a fast pace, getting involved in every game in the playground and running from one activity to another. He can barely sit still. He's kinaesthetic, sporty and process-orientated. When his teacher asks him whether he wants to play football or build with Lego this afternoon he has no idea. He wants to do both and he can't decide. He doesn't answer and the teacher gets cross because he hasn't

(Contd)

CASE STUDY

answered her question, but he isn't being rude, he just wants to be told what to do and doesn't want to make a choice.

Jenny loves to spend her time in the playground deciding who to play with and what games to play. She enjoys the options and thinks playtime is such fun because she could play with the skipping ropes with Georgia or tag with Josie or in the home corner with Maia or go on the climbing frame with Tom. When the teacher asks her to play hopscotch with Ahsan, she is cross because her choices have been taken away. If the teacher had asked her to *choose* a game to play with Ahsan, she would have happily done so.

AWAY FROM/TOWARDS

Some children are naturally risk averse and go through life making decisions that will be safe choices that avoid conflict or imagined (or real) threats. You will know how you are yourself, but if your child is just like you, you may not have noticed that this is their preferred style. Does your child talk about what they *want* or what they do not want? Although it is perfectly OK for them to choose this, they may need a bit of encouragement sometimes to verbalize what they *do* want and this is generally a healthier attitude that will help them achieve what they want.

For example, if your child says 'I don't want to eat that' (familiar words maybe), it may be difficult for them to say what they *do* want. Play the game and ask what else they do not want to eat, because that is their preferred zone, and then provide something they haven't mentioned on the basis that they don't 'not want' it. Emphasize the positive choice: 'So you do want a burger, then?'

PROACTIVE/REACTIVE

Similar to the above is the desire some of us have to react to things rather than be the instigator. In communication it can be hard to encourage children to start a conversation or make a decision, take responsibility or initiate an activity. They tend to look to someone else, often you, when they are small, to start the ball rolling. If this becomes a habit later in life they will find it hard to lead others in team exercises or in the workplace. Encourage them to contribute their ideas and therefore take responsibility for the outcome. For example:

You	What shall we do today? Shall we go to the park and take a ball or would you like to feed the ducks?
Child	Feed the ducks.
You	What a good idea of yours to feed the ducks. You get the bread and I'll find a bag to put it in.

In this section we've talked about how to communicate better with our children by matching their body language, way of speaking, language styles, way of processing information and making decisions. If we communicate with them in the way they find easiest, then misunderstandings happen rarely and you will be able to achieve the clear communication that makes for good rapport and a great relationship.

Negotiating skills

Of course we're all looking for a win-win in negotiations with our children but let's face it, if we can't get that we still want to get our own way because we are the parents and we know best. But is this what it's all about, getting our own way? If we have rapport with our child, a win-win situation is much easier to achieve.

Let's just recap how to develop rapport with our child.

When talking with children you should get down to their physical level – that immediately helps you communicate. By matching facial expressions and hand gestures, we connect non-verbally. Children express themselves freely and more clearly through their facial expressions than their words, especially when they are very young. By mimicking them we can better understand what they want to communicate. Matching tone of voice, pitch, volume, rhythm and body language not only enables you to really get into their shoes and see the world as they see it, but also puts you in a position of strength because once they see you are 'with them' in spirit you can steer them towards where you want them to be or what you want them to do. Once you have the rapport it is then easier to take over control if they want something they can't have.

Here's an example. Your child won't do his homework and every discussion ends with stalemate because your child simply doesn't want to do it now. Open up the desired outcome big-chunk and the compromise might be to do it at a different time altogether. My son does his homework with no problem in the car on the way to school, not ideal you may say, but it achieves the desired outcome of getting it done and is acceptable to both of us.

Be aware, too, of how your child looks at the world. We've just mentioned big-chunk and small-chunk to cover whether they like general or detailed discussions. Some children are away-from and some are towards, so when negotiating, choose options that recognize this preference. A towards child will want to have a positive goal, for example, doing his homework so he can stay ahead in the class, but an away-from child would be more motivated by doing his homework so he doesn't get told off. Some children thrive on choice whereas others prefer process. Give them what they need. When negotiating with a child who likes choices offer a choice of when to do what you want them to do, before or after tea, in this room or that room, with you or on their own. A child who prefers process will prefer to know what needs doing and work through it without options, which distract.

FILTERS AND NEGOTIATION

Deletions, distortions and generalizations can have a negative effect on negotiation.

An example of deletion would be to say, 'Other children are better in class because they do their homework', but *which* 'other children' and *how* are they 'better'?

Distortions are when we say things like, '*You make me* angry when you don't clean up your room' or '*You're* trying to annoy me.' The reality is that you have *chosen* to be angry, and as you are not a mind-reader you can't say why your child is doing something. These sorts of things are better expressed as, 'I feel angry when you don't tidy your room' or 'I feel annoyed when you say that.'

Generalizations are when we use words like 'always', 'never' and 'everyone'; these are almost never true and looking at the *exceptions* can bring to light the solutions. 'My child *never* does what I want them to do.' Never? When *do* they do what you want them to do?

Some of the things we say to children when trying to negotiate can have the opposite effect; others can seriously damage their self-esteem.

I think we all know how upset children get when they are called 'stupid' and the result of name calling tends to be that the child is labelled 'stupid' in their own mind and behaves accordingly. This is so with other labels like 'fat' or 'lazy', 'selfish' and so on. Instead, find an example of the opposite positive behaviour and remind them that they have the ability to behave in that way. Blaming and accusing children tends to result in them feeling bad about themselves and doesn't result in a 'win-win' but a 'lose-lose'. If your child has done something wrong, stolen some money from your purse for example, give them the option to own up and return the money and tell them how you *feel* about it. Remind them of times when they have been honest and truthful.

Threatening children is a form of bullying that they will model, so we must avoid this, although it can be tempting when our backs are against the wall! Instead, we can tell children stories reminding them of their resources. For example, rather than threaten a child who is running around the supermarket, say, 'I know a little girl who walks really nicely with me in the supermarket, a really helpful little girl like she was the other day when she found me the baby wipes when I couldn't find them. I wonder where she is today?' The chances are that she will say 'I'm here Mummy, what can I help you find today?' There is no need to bribe them with things to negotiate; children *want* to please you, have time with you and for you to love them.

Sarcasm doesn't work with children as they don't understand it until they are in their teens. It is humiliating for them as it is a language they don't speak and sounds unkind. Even just saying 'You've done it again, dropped the jam jar, brilliant!' may not sound like sarcasm, but it is and children feel stupid and unloved. This sort of talk can lead to poor self-esteem and this is so unnecessary when what they need is reassurance.

You don't know what the future will hold for them so prophesying is again unhelpful in negotiating. For example, 'You won't have any friends if you go about punching people' may sound reasonable to you, but what they need to know is, 'I think your friends would like you if you didn't hurt them.'

Tip

When negotiating with children or teens, let them know you love them and together you will find a 'win-win' solution to the situation you need to resolve.

▶ Place three chairs facing each other and sit in one. That chair represents you.

▶ Use the other chair to represent your child or the person with whom you are having a problem. The third chair represents an outside or objective person sitting in on the discussion.

▶ Say what you want to say to the chair representing your child and then switch chairs and respond as your child. Switch back to respond and so on until you've said all you wish to say and have responded as your child.

▶ Then go and sit in the chair representing the outside person and respond to all you've seen and heard. Hopefully you have reframed the situation now.

Show your child how to do this exercise because it's a great resource for all sorts of negotiating and encourages them to see things from another perspective.

The negotiating skills that you model for your children will prove very useful for them as they go through life and the younger you start showing them how to do it, the more uses they will find for it.

Giving and receiving support

We all want to give our children support throughout their lives and we in turn will need to be able to ask for support, but most of us are better at giving than receiving, aren't we? How, though, can you constantly give out if you yourself are not supported?

Other people are not very good at guessing what we need until it is too late. Even good friends and family sometimes miss the danger signs and we can find ourselves doing harm through drink or drugs, abusive behaviour, not eating or over eating, anything really to get the attention we need. We must learn, before it is too late, how to ask for help. If you can teach this to your children when they are very young, they will be well-armed for those vulnerable teenage years ahead.

So how do we learn to ask for help? Let's first reframe it as giving someone we care about the opportunity to give us support. On the basis that we like to help and care about them, it seems fair to assume that they want to reciprocate. We sometimes end up doing far more than we can cope with because we reason that it will take too long to explain what we want to someone else, or that it may not be done as we want, and sometimes we actually want to be in control so we get all the reward and praise for the achievement.

Put yourself in someone else's shoes, doesn't it feel good to be asked for help? Isn't it more fun to share a task and work with other people? It feels good to give, whether it is a present, a compliment or our affection. Denying someone this by trying to cope on your own has a pay-off. What pay-off are we getting for coping on our own and turning the help away? Do we feel grown up, independent and able to cope on our own? Or is it that we can't relinquish control? We often encourage children to do things themselves to become more independent, but do we subconsciously also teach them that to ask for help is a sign of failure?

We can *model* asking for help so that children learn not only how to do it but also that it is not a sign of weakness. For example:

> *'Charlie, could you just help Mummy brush Cocoa? It's quite hard to do it on my own. I don't seem to have enough hands. Please could you stroke his head so I can brush underneath it? Thank you. It's great to do things together; it makes it much easier.'*

> *'Sophie, please could you answer the phone for me if Grandma rings and tell her we're on our way. I just have to get the cases in the car. Tom, please could you take the other side of this heavy bag with me? Thank you, that's such a great help.'*

You can also prompt *them* to ask for help, for example:

Child	I can't do up my laces.
You	Well, how do you ask me nicely?
Child	Mummy, please could you help me with my laces?
You	Yes of course, let me show you.

Although it may seem relatively easy to give support compared with asking for help, NLP has some helpful new skills on offer. One fairly recent development in NLP has been what we call 'clean language'. It refers to total unconditional respect for what the other person is saying and desire to understand their point of view as if you are in their shoes and experiencing their world and not projecting your own 'stuff' onto it.

We can apply the same principles as with rapport by using the same words as the person we want to help, then add on to it by using the words 'and in what way...?'

Let's say your son or daughter has come home from school upset by something that had happened in the playground that day. We would naturally listen to their account of what had happened and comfort them. But there's more you can do using NLP:

Child	Mummy, Phoebe told me she didn't want to be my friend anymore and I'm so sad.
You	Phoebe told you she didn't want to be your friend anymore? And in what way do you feel sad?
Child	I won't have anyone to play with at break time and I really like Phoebe.
You	You won't have anyone to play with at break time, and in what way do you really like Phoebe?
Child	She's my only friend.
You	In what way is Phoebe your only friend?
Child	Well, she isn't my only friend, I like Anya as well. I suppose I could play with her... and Flora... and I like Alice too.

By respecting your child's feelings and echoing them, this invites them to open themselves up to new possibilities. If you had responded differently, perhaps suggesting other friends she could play with or reminding her that Phoebe wasn't her only friend a few weeks ago, your child might feel belittled, take a more defensive stance and feel sadder about a situation she can resolve herself, with your support.

If we recognize that we all have the resources to solve our problems, our role as a support is about helping them find that resource within themselves and helping them feel confident to ask for the help they need.

You can give support by listening out for and challenging generalizations, deletions and distortions. Here are some examples of these:

Generalizations are when we use words like 'always' or 'never' when we don't mean it literally, such as, 'I never get a part in the school play' or 'The teacher always picks on me.' It may feel like this, but rarely is. Point out the exceptions so they see the positives, i.e. remind them of the time they did get a part, or when their teacher said nice things about them.

Other generalizations are 'everyone', 'no one' and 'every', suggesting that this is a universal truth when it isn't. Does your child sometimes tell you that 'no one' played with him at playtime or that 'everyone' has the latest collectible cards?

Distortions can take the form of 'mind reading', assumptions and not taking responsibility for our own feelings but rather blaming others for them. An example of mind reading is when we say things like 'I know you don't want to...' or 'I know you think...' Are you sure you know this or are you just guessing?

Assumptions are when we think we are privy to the feelings of others, such as 'You must feel...' or 'He must be furious.' Remember, however close you are to someone, it's usually best to check out assumptions we have. In NLP terms, we call that being 'ecological'.

When we say, 'You make me cross' or 'Why did you make me angry?' or 'Why did you make your sister cry?', this is an example of not taking responsibility for the choices we make to feel how we feel. No one can actually make us angry; we have chosen to be angry or sad or happy. It would be cleaner language to say, 'I felt really angry when you said that.'

Deletions are when we make a comparative statement without specifying the reference, such as 'It's better to do what I say.'

When children come out with these deletions, distortions and generalizations, they are asking for support and reassurance that the situation isn't as bad as it seems. They want us to find the exceptions. So the next time your child says, 'I always get my words muddled up' point out that she didn't just then! Look for the positive exception.

Another very interesting linguistic pattern in NLP is called 'embedded commands'. How often do we call out to a child, 'You'll drop that' as they struggle with something too heavy for them? What happens next? They drop it! We have effectively given them an embedded command.

Have you heard the expression 'Don't think about pink elephants!'? We can't *not* think about something! Our mind has to conjure up pink elephants so we know what it is we mustn't think about.

Instead, if we said nothing, or something supportive such as 'You're being very careful with that chair, well done' they will be extra careful and be less likely to drop it. We must learn to give our children positive suggestions.

> **Tip**
> Giving and receiving support is about using rapport and modelling skills, underpinned by the NLP belief that we have the resources we need. This includes the resource of asking for help.

Embracing change

If you're reading this book it is because you are willing to make some changes. Perhaps what you are currently doing doesn't work as well as you'd like so you are open to new ideas.

Before we talk about change, we should look at where our ideas and expectations have come from. They have come from our *environment*.

Our ideas on parenting come from many sources: our own parents and carers, books and magazines, TV programmes and, of course, our friends and loved ones.

Use this space here to jot down ten things that come to mind without too much thought, in answer to this question: What do you consider to be a 'good parent?'

A 'good parent' is someone who:

1

2

3

4

5

6

7

8

9

10

Now go back and write down alongside each of these answers, where that belief came from. Did it come from your own parents or grandparents, from seeing your friends or older siblings as parents, from the TV or what you've read?

You can choose whether or not you want to hold on to and accept these beliefs. Release yourself from beliefs that don't belong to you or to your own environment. Go back and cross any out that are holding you back because they are not your own beliefs but handed to you by others.

Ideas on parenting are constantly changing and we are often fascinated by these new ideas – anything that will make the difference we are looking for. We latch on to them, experiment and maybe for a while they work.

It is important to establish for yourself what is working well in your parenting. What are you excellent at? If your friends were to comment on you as a parent, what would they agree that you do well? The trouble is that we are rather too ready to criticize ourselves, find fault and focus on the negative aspects of anything.

NLP as a theory has at its heart a positive beat. You will find that all the tools explained and discussed throughout this book focus on the good intention, learning from what we do well, and bringing it across from one part of our lives to where it's needed. NLP principles are about looking for the positive, desired outcome in our interactions with our children, not the avoidance of a negative outcome.

So before we continue, please use this space to write down what works. What are you good at and what brings you joy in the relationship you have with your children? Remember to word these thoughts in a positive way, for example, 'He doesn't throw tantrums in the supermarket' becomes 'He is well behaved when we go out.' Sometimes listing the positive can be quite an eye-opener because it can show you helpful patterns.

Things I am good at as a parent:

1

2

3

4

5

6

7

8

Is the list longer than you anticipated? Is there anything you've written that has surprised you?

It's not unusual to react to 'bad behaviour' and hardly notice the good behaviour. Why is that?

In a way, we expect good behaviour from our children even though this is totally unreasonable, unless of course you are completely perfect. We are prone to mood swings because of circumstances, PMT, stress at work and at home. We feel the need for more attention than we are getting and we often feel overwhelmed by the responsibilities of being a parent, especially if we are doing this on our own. Yet, as adults we have some coping mechanisms and we know that the difficult times won't last forever; we can also verbalize our worries and stress to caring friends and family. Imagine just for a moment that you are a five-year-old child and suddenly you are in a classroom with lots of children you don't know and you can't see Mummy. She's told you all about school, but you can't remember because you feel so confused and alone. Usually Mummy is there to cuddle you when you want to cry but she isn't here now.

Don't we all remember that first day at 'big school'; it's not just the children who cry, is it? Round the corner from the school gates is a gaggle of parents trying to be brave, sitting in their cars and sniffling into their mobile phone to their friend or partner. How will you get through the day until you see them again?

It is important to hold on to that sense of your inner child, your raw feelings and emotions, those overwhelming feelings of confusion, and then remember them when your child behaves 'badly' and try to crawl into their world to find out what's happening for them.

THE IMPORTANCE OF PATTERNS

Look for patterns of behaviour. Some children behave differently with Mum than with Dad. Some behave better at school, better at friends' houses, better in the morning and so on.

Noticing patterns of behaviour

Keep a diary over the course of a week and note at each hour of the day what you notice about your child's behaviour, then transfer the most repeated behaviours here so that you can see the patterns emerging:

First thing in the morning:

Mid-morning:

Midday:

Afternoon:

Early evening:

Later evening:

Another pattern to consider is your own state of mind. Sometimes identical behaviour can result in completely different responses from us. If we are tired, for example, we will respond quite differently to a bit of a prank at bedtime and it is no wonder that children get confused and wonder what they've done wrong. They haven't done anything wrong. We have simply been inconsistent and given mixed messages. Does the better behaviour and relationship happen when you are less tired, less stressed, at different times of the month, when you feel sexually frustrated, hungry and so on? What can you learn from it?

We need to be consistent. If a child receives a gentle reprimand for doing something one week, and a serious telling off for the same misdemeanour the following week, he is going to harbour feelings of resentment and injustice towards you.

If you are prepared to make changes, look at what your child eats alongside the patterns you have observed. Low blood sugar at about 4 pm when your child hasn't eaten since lunchtime can account for many a mad half hour! Try making a small snack for them to eat in the car on the way home or, if you have a short journey, give them something nutritious rather than a chocolate or sweet bar that just gives them a sugar high without any sustained energy boost. Similarly, a milky drink at bedtime can just fill the tummy enough to settle them for the night without the sugar high of food.

If all this seems rather harsh and you are worried that your child will think you're being unkind, you can find other nice treats to replace the sweets, such as a new comic, trip to the park or other fun thing that has a positive effect on behaviour. After all, they want positive attention not negative attention.

Other patterns you see may be more about lack of exercise. Boys need loads of exercise. A headteacher of a boys' school has said, 'Boys are like puppies; you need to let them outside to tear around for a while then you can teach them a little. Then let them outside again to get rid of their energy before any more work. It's impossible to teach a bouncing puppy or a bouncing boy.' It is the same thing with parenting. If your child has been cooped up at school all day with little exercise or fresh air (and this happens a lot in the winter) they will have loads of pent-up energy and may misbehave out of sheer physical frustration.

This tends to be more noticeable when you have your second child and you want your older child to be careful, not run around because they might knock over the toddler, and you yourself will be tired and not so willing to go for walks, trips to the park, swimming pool and so on.

There are lots of ways, even nowadays when we are so conscious of the safety of our children, for them to let off steam. Local sports clubs will be a great outlet with the additional benefit of your child having a new group of friends, opportunities to learn social skills, getting a chance to be part of a team, compete and achieve outside of school. Equally, leisure centres run after-school activities such as sports, trampolining and so on. For the younger child there are toddler activity groups, swimming classes and so on.

Tip

Most people have access to a garden or local park and a trip there before and after school is a great way for children to let off steam, get a good oxygen boost to the brain before school and a good chance to relax and unwind after school.

Exercise releases all those happy hormones – endorphins – and a child who seems listless or even a bit depressed can cheer up enormously when they run about chasing a ball or playing with the dog. You too! If you're going through a hard time in your relationship or with another child, instead of brooding on it at home, go out for a run or a cycle and you may well find the situation seems much more positive.

Tip

Exercise and diet have huge effects on children's bodies. Take a good look at the list of behavioural patterns you made on p. 74. Look again for patterns in behaviour as a result of their diet and exercise habits and make changes accordingly.

You may think all this is rather obvious and of course it is. But the reason these thoughts on patterns have been included is to show you how seemingly minor changes can make a difference. The following chapters of the book focus on situations that occur in parenting and how NLP can help. If you are already looking for patterns, you will be better able to notice positive changes you make using NLP.

4

Time management

In this chapter you will learn:
- *how to value yourself and your time*
- *how to find 'me time' in the hurly burly of family life*
- *when and how to say 'no'*
- *prioritizing and delegating*

How good are you at time management? As parents, we are constantly watching the time because we have to pack so much into every day. There are lots more things to think about when you have children and there never seem to be enough hours in the day.

This chapter won't give you more hours in the day but it *will* give you the skills to manage your time better by weighing up priorities against your values and by learning to delegate.

NLP has a lovely expression, 'living in the moment'. It isn't exclusive to NLP of course. Many philosophers and religious leaders have spoken about the importance of living in the moment. We know it in our hearts, don't we, but we just wonder whether those who go on about it are actually working parents!

This is about being happy to just stand still and enjoy the moment rather than dwell on what has just happened or be thinking ahead to what is about to happen. Oprah Winfrey sums up the essence so succinctly.

> *Living in the moment brings you a sense of reverence for all of life's blessings.*
>
> Oprah Winfrey

The idea of living in the moment is based on time line theory, which was covered in the last chapter so here is a quick recap.

Time line exercise

Imagine a line on the floor and find the place that represents today. Looking back along the line, take one step at a time into the past. Now turn around and look back at today – what does your life today look like, one step back into the past?

Maybe the first step back is before you had children or when you were working in a particular job, or before you met your partner.

If you're visual, as you've taken that step back are you seeing yourself and the people around you? If you are *seeing* this place on your time line as a film or series of photographs, then you are visual so enjoy the show!

If you are hearing voices from the past, listening to people talking, hearing music you used to listen to, the sound of the workplace or something like that, then you are auditory.

You're kinaesthetic if your thoughts are around feelings, being warm or cold, comfortable or uncomfortable and if you're remembering emotions rather than images or sounds. You could well be experiencing a combination of these three but usually one will dominate and for this exercise concentrate on the dominant one.

If you have decided that you are visual, stand on the time line and walk back in time stopping at each point to see the images in your mind. Really zoom in on them, turn up the colour, sharpen the focus and explore the images so you are in them. This is called *associating*.

If you are auditory, find the tone control and the volume knob and play with the sound until it is crystal clear and loud.

If you are kinaesthetic, really feel those feelings as if they were happening right now.

Once you've done this exercise in your past, step off the line and 'break state'. What I mean by that is, do something completely different for a moment. It can be quite emotional stepping back into the past and you may want to just take a break and think about something else. Once you've done this and feel relaxed, step back to today's point on the line.

You will probably have a different feeling about today, more acute, more focused and more definitely in the moment especially if going back in time helped you slay a few dragons and get your perspective about the past into its context.

Where are you today? What are the emotions you are feeling, the images you see in your mind and the sounds you are hearing? What's positive and good about today's place on the line? You may want to note these down so you can look at them when you don't feel so great.

Now take a step forward to a point ahead of you on the line. What does that represent for you? This could be relating to your work, children, your relationship or a life-changing event such as moving house. Take yourself into that time and what it might feel like. You will probably have a sense of change and progress that would take you towards the next point in the line. If you do, then move to it now and experience that next point. Continue to move forward on the line in the same way, achieving new changes in your life. Try to stay at each point on the line long enough to really see, hear and feel what that position means to you.

Now go back to today's place and think about what you need to do today to make the next move along the line. How does today look now you have some experience of the next step?

Many people who do this exercise find that today becomes much clearer, more vivid and more positive because they can see that it is a step in a direction rather than a point with no future.

This exercise, however silly it may at first appear as you walk along this imaginary line, can actually be very grounding and positive. It helps you realize that whatever negative things you may be experiencing now are just phases or brief moments in time. Your children grow up, life decisions become clearer and choices you make now will enable future goals to be reached.

Valuing your time

Valuing your time is also about valuing yourself as an individual. It's easy to lose sight of yourself as you juggle all your responsibilities as a parent.

What are your values, what is important to you as an individual? What do you need in your life in order for it to have meaning and purpose? Quickly write down your thoughts on what is important to you. Some people find that it is easier to say what they don't want but this is again 'away from' thinking, so make these thoughts 'towards' thinking.

Here are some suggestions for how you might phrase your values:

▶ A day is a good day if I have time to...
▶ I feel happy if I get a chance to...
▶ I would like to have more time to...
▶ What really makes me happy is...
▶ My perfect day is when I can...
▶ If I could do whatever I wanted today I would...
▶ If only I could...
▶ One day I will...
▶ When I have some spare time I will...

Think about what makes for a good day. Is it a combination or balance that makes it a good day or is there one particular thing that makes it a good day, such as if your baby goes down for a nap or if your toddler eats their lunch or your child does their homework without being nagged? Share your thoughts on this with your family. They *want* you to have a good day so perhaps you can help your child have a good day at the same time. Sometimes by discussing your values you will find that a compromise can be reached which enables everyone to have a good day.

Have a go

1 Using the sentences suggested above, make a list of your values now.
2 Look at each item on the list and ask yourself, 'What can I do differently to achieve this value in my life?'

DAY TO DAY LIFE

Every moment of the day, you are making choices or going through processes. Some people are more aware than others of the choices they can make and weigh up the options at each one. Others go through the day mentally ticking off what needs to be done. Are you a choices person or a process person? Could you benefit from considering that you do have choices if you are a process person or if you are a choices person could you benefit from limiting some of the choices and just getting on with what needs to be done?

Do you have a goal for each day (towards thinking) or do you go through the day trying to avoid disaster (away-from thinking)? The important thing is to make the most of the day. As you go through the day, think about how you could make the most of the time. Value yourself and your own needs. Of course you have children to take care of, but could you do it in a way that will be enjoyable to you? You do have choices and can exercise them. What do you want to get out of the day? What is your goal, what positive outcome do you want?

Do you have a friend who seems to do this well? Someone who seems to have the balance right and make time for themselves? If so, ask them how they do it. Watch and learn from someone who seems to make choices you'd like to make. This is another example of modelling in NLP. How easy it is to observe other mums or dads and think 'how do they do it?' Instead of thinking 'I can't do that' think 'How can I do that too?' Check out their secret. You may have to ask several people what their secret is because their solution may not work for you, but it may be that the tenth person you ask has a secret that will work.

Think about the choices you make though the day. What if you made a different choice? What possibilities are there? A really good phrase to make part of your daily mantra is 'What if I could...?' Instead of thinking 'I can't...' or 'I wish I could...', replace this with '*And what if I could?*' This will open up all sorts of possibilities for you. Visualize the possibilities and imagine yourself doing them. If you can visualize achieving what you want, you are well on the way to achieving it.

If you value yourself and your personal goals, what makes for a good day and what makes you happy, your positivity will show itself to others. You will draw people to you because positive people give off an energy that others want to share. The reverse is also true that if you don't value yourself and your time, others will take advantage of you and won't respect you or your needs.

Prioritizing

In order to value your time you will need to make choices and this requires you to *prioritize*. Each choice you make will come down to what you value most at that time.

Do it, dump it or delegate it.

In most cases, these are the only three decisions. Most mums and dads just 'do it' because they don't see any other way but not everything has to be done; some things can be dumped or delegated. If you are someone who crams too much into the day and ends up exhausted and feeling resentful, then you need to re-evaluate your priorities.

Have a go

1 Make a list of everything you do on a daily basis.
2 Now go back through it, and looking at each item decide whether you could dump it.

Consider: does this item have value for you? Is it part of your identity, something totally intrinsic to your role that makes you feel you have a meaningful existence? If it is, then keep doing it.

If it gives you no pleasure, does not contribute towards your values or identity and is not fundamental to your beliefs about how you should live your life, then *dump it*. If you're not sure, then ask yourself:

▶ If I did not do this task, what would happen?
▶ How would I feel about myself if I did not complete it?
▶ Would I feel a failure as a person?
▶ If I didn't do it, what *could* I do instead?

If you are satisfied that your answers to the above mean that you could dump the item, then cross it off your list and go on to the next one.

3 Keep going until you just have the 'do it' list. Hopefully your list has shortened.
4 Now add to the 'do it' list something from your values list you completed on pp. 28–9. Add something that makes you happy,

SAYING 'NO'

Learning to say no is a skill that some parents need to learn. PTAs,
committees and voluntary organisations are full of busy parents, often
mothers, who can't say no. Obviously if no one said yes, we'd have
no Brownies and Beavers, school fetes and other crucial fundraising
activities which enable our children to have activities they enjoy. We
need to '**bridge the gap**', another NLP concept. Instead of automatically
saying 'yes' when someone asks you to do something, say, 'Let me
think about it and get back to you.' You may well come back to them
with a yes, but at least let the suggestion go through some thought
process so you can work out *how* you can do it, whether it meets your
value criteria, whether you can *dump* or *delegate* something else in
order to do it and whether it is within your skill set or desired skill set.

You need to be able to pass on the skill of prioritizing to your
children as they reach the age of having exams, coursework deadlines
and increasing demands on their time. When they are very young,
they live in the moment and don't need to think ahead – you will
probably be doing that on their behalf.

Older children need to learn to weigh up what is important and what
they have to do, what they can dump and what they can delegate.
Chances are that *you* will be the person they try to delegate all the
jobs they didn't want to do in the first place, such as household
chores, tidying their bedroom, walking the dog and so on. This is
where your bridging the gap strategy will come in handy because
you may want to agree to picking up something they're delegating
for a fixed period of time, such as during exam revision, but want to
negotiate with them to make up for it after the exams are finished by
them doing more jobs then.

Prioritizing skills are very important in work life and home life
and are based on the principle that not everything has to be done;

some things have more priority because they meet a value need for you. Others that don't can be dumped or delegated.

Coping with guilt

Let's face it, motherhood and guilt go hand in hand. Mothers probably never had these feelings with such intensity before having children. Not only do they tend to feel guilty where there could conceivably be reason to, but they also take on guilt feelings when the situation has absolutely nothing to do with them. Why is that?

Girls tend to be more sociable than boys. Where boys chase each other and play-fight with sticks, girls huddle in the corner chatting. Girls want to be liked, they want to be popular and they want to be helpful and supportive. They grow into caring and loving mothers who would do anything for their children, friends and family. It's not that men don't, of course they want to do these things, but from the time we all lived in caves, women have been programmed to nurture and men have been programmed to hunt and protect, so nurturing does not generally come as easily to them nor is it the first response.

As soon as we cannot do something or feel we have fallen short of expectations we feel guilty. We *choose* to feel guilty, in NLP terms. According to NLP we can choose how we feel. This can be quite a hard concept to take on board at first. What it means, though, is that while it may be justifiable to feel guilty if we have not acted according to our values, we don't have to choose to feel guilty for *everything*.

Bridge the gap

When you are about to choose a guilty feeling:

1 STOP
2 Think:
   ▶ Is this really my fault?
   ▶ Did I do it?
   ▶ Was it my responsibility to do it?
3 If the answers are 'NO' then choose another feeling. Choose instead, perhaps, a sympathetic response or a helpful suggestion.
4 If the answers are 'YES' then apologize, learn from it and move on, because holding on to guilt can be hugely limiting.

Guilt gets us in touch with our feelings and serves a purpose in that way. It can help us prioritize because it is a 'wake-up call' that we are doing too much when we should focus and be more aware of our responsibilities. If your guilt can be addressed by taking on less, working less and changing a behaviour, then it has served a useful purpose. If there is or was nothing you could have done differently to avoid the situation which has caused you to feel guilty, then this is *regret* rather than guilt.

The worst guilt is probably associated with those we feel most responsibility for, such as babies and small children. Small children frequently have accidents because they run about without looking where they are going, climb higher than is safe and have no fear because they still think the world is a safe place. It is our job to ensure that their world is as safe as we can make it, for example, using stair gates to protect them from the stairs and the kitchen, ensuring garden gates are locked and windows are not left open and so on. We try to watch them all the time and of course in some situations, such as near water, it is essential that they are watched all the time. But accidents can happen in seconds and can be completely impossible to foresee. Parents do feel guilty because they are responsible for the safety of their young children, but instead of letting the guilt completely overcome you, better instead to be solution-focused and learn from the experience.

Lots of parents feel guilty about the time or money that they can't spend on their children because of work or other pressures. If you can't change this then accept the situation with regret and make the most of what time is available. Although the term 'quality time' has become rather hackneyed, we all recognize what that means and want to enjoy time with our children doing something fun that they will value. Children love to have new toys, video games and clothes, but this doesn't match the value of time with them; it is usually just distraction therapy for our guilty feelings so we can put a smile on their face for a moment.

Children need boundaries and need to have limits on pocket money, gifts and behaviour. It is not necessary to feel guilty about setting boundaries and being a good parent, quite the reverse. If you explain the boundaries and rules and why they have been set, this makes them clear about what is expected of them and what they can expect of you. This also makes it easier to accept rules and boundaries when they start school, and to behave and speak to other adults in an acceptable way.

Guilt tends to happen when people feel that they have not met other people's expectations. When you let go of the guilt, you can be a more relaxed parent.

Guilt over working or not working can seem insupportable because no matter what we choose, we feel we could do better. We don't have the freedom to make our own preferred choice on account of other factors beyond our control such as the cost of living and childcare, lack of well-paid part-time work opportunities and so on. This is *regret* though, not guilt, because we don't have the responsibility or the control over these aspects of our life.

As children get older it becomes more important that parents model independence, good work ethic, budget management and how to handle decision-making, so involving them in these decisions helps them grow in maturity and respect you for your choices. Life is all about balancing what *needs* to be done and what you *want* to do, and how better to demonstrate that to children than by your own example. You have your own needs as an individual and when they can see how you have to balance those with your responsibilities as a parent and your financial demands, they can apply this to competing pressures at difficult times such as exams and work.

Be confident about the choices you make and communicate them so that others understand and support you. There is no reason to feel guilty; you are making the best decisions you can for your family.

'Me time'

'What is that?' you ask! Yes, for many this might be a foreign concept. For some it may be difficult to remember who 'me' is. We pack our lives with hundreds of jobs we have to do, work, kids, our own parents, pets and other responsibilities and often end up with not only no time for ourselves but we are often too tired to do anything anyway.

What did you used to enjoy doing? Use the time line to remind yourself.

Remember that NLP thinking assures us that we have the resources to do whatever we want – if we can find someone who does have 'me time' we can model them or we can look for the resource in other parts of our lives.

Let's look at our own resources first. Can you think of a time or situation in your life when you had to squeeze in something that you didn't really have time for? Perhaps you did your homework in the car going to school, on the bus or while you ate breakfast? Did you delegate work in your job so you could find the time to do something you couldn't delegate? If you did anything like that then you do have the resources to make 'me time'.

Find opportunities when you can do something for yourself. If you are reading this and thinking 'I can't find the time', think again. Are you valuing yourself enough? A good parent is a happy parent and you'll be happier if you value yourself and give yourself love as well as your child. Depriving ourselves of 'me time' makes us feel sad and undervalued but the only person who can give you this time is *you*.

Of course if your partner will take the baby so you can have a nice relaxing bath and a read, time to shop on your own or time with a friend, then that's great but you may have to *ask* for this. How good are you at asking for things for yourself?

Let's do an exercise in self-esteem here.

Disassociation exercise

If you are suffering from low self-esteem, it's easy to only see the negatives. We have to stand back and disassociate – pretend we are someone else looking at us. What can they see?

1 Look at yourself through their eyes. Work your way down from top to toe and take in all that someone else can see.
2 Whenever you see anything negative, look again and see that thing from someone else's viewpoint. Perhaps they don't see that thing at all. See the whole you. If they didn't know you, what impression might they have of you as a person? What would they like about you?
3 Imagine you have some controls that can make some parts of you brighter or sharper and more focused. If you like music, select a track as backing for your image. Play with the lighting as if you were setting up the best photo of you that you could possibly imagine.
4 When the photo is at that point when you would be happy for anyone to take the photo, 'anchor' it by clicking the button on your imaginary camera.
5 Break state by deliberately thinking of something else.
6 Now take the pose again. Look your best, smile, feel good about yourself, then step away and look at yourself as if you were someone else looking and taking the photo. Click again.

Do this a few times until you have anchored that great feeling. You need to be able to access that feeling or 'drop the anchor' whenever you need a boost of self-esteem that allows you to ask for the help you need to spend some 'me time'.

Now that you're feeling good about yourself let's reinforce that with some questions.

▶ Do you like yourself?
▶ Are you a good human being?
▶ Do you deserve to be loved?
▶ Do you deserve happiness?
▶ Do you deserve 'me time'?

Hopefully the answer to all of them was a resounding 'YES'. Now use your juggling and delegation skills to make sure you get that 'me time'!

Delegating

It's the hardest thing to delegate any aspect of parenting because we tend to feel that it's *our* job, don't we?

Delegating requires trust. We need to learn to trust that someone else can do the things that we feel only *we* can do best. After all, it's our own child and we know best, right? But sometimes we have to trust because we simply can't do everything ourselves.

Who do you trust and what is there about that person that means they can be trusted? Do you trust your family because they have a blood link to your child? Do you trust professionals because they have relevant training and experience? Do you trust people who are paid to do a job because they have a responsibility? What does trust mean to you?

What are *you* trusted to do and what makes others trust you? What have you had to prove or show others for you to be worthy of their trust?

When you delegate a task there is always some degree of latitude because the person to whom you are delegating it may interpret the task differently. Their values may be different from yours, their beliefs will probably be different and their environment may also be different, which will affect how they do what you have asked.

Communication is key. When you delegate, make sure you identify the important aspects of the task, giving them all the information they need. Delegation involves letting go and taking a risk, not something we generally feel comfortable with if it's our own child. Yet we do take risks every day and if we didn't, our children would be so wrapped in cotton wool that they'd be cocooned from the environment and unable to cope with taking responsibility for themselves. It is, of course, harder to take a risk with a baby or toddler who can't express themselves clearly. We've all had babysitters tell us that our child told them a completely different bedtime than we did.

We tend to over-control our children out of fear of the risks they might encounter, so we persuade ourselves that it is for their own good. But even the logic behind our actions can be questionable.

For example, we might control children most when they are likely to encounter strangers, and yet the fact remains that most abuse happens by people already known to the children, and *not* from strangers.

Delegation and trust take time to learn and you need to start gradually. Encourage your child to do simple things for themselves, however long it takes and however exasperating! Just taking time to show them how to tie shoelaces, for example, will give them self-confidence in their abilities at a very simple level.

In the Montessori system of learning, children spend their early years before formal education learning to fold, tie, do up buttons, pour and spoon in order to build the essential gross motor skills. They need these skills for writing but these basics are also useful in fending for themselves. They are taught to tidy away, replace their chair at the table, eat with a knife and fork and basic everyday courtesies such as apologizing and owning up to misdemeanours. Nowadays, teachers have to teach these skills at a much later age because some parents have not already done this. By training children in these simple life skills you are *delegating* tasks to them that give them confidence.

Tip

The Montessori way of teaching a child to put on their coat or jacket is as follows. The child lays out their coat on the floor with the outside of the coat on the floor side, facing away from them. Then they reach down and put their arms in the opposite arms of the coat and flip it over their head. Job done! If you buy them a coat with large buttons or a zip they can do it up as well!

Delegating to another adult works in a similar way. Patience is essential as you show or explain to someone what needs to be done and watch and help them do it initially.

Communicating to either a child or an adult to whom you are delegating requires *rapport*. You can apply what we have already learned about the way we prefer to communicate so you *match* the words to the other person's preferred style. If you are delegating to someone who has a visual preference, write down what needs to be done or show them how to do it. An auditory person needs to be *told* and they will remember, and a kinaesthetic person needs to be shown as well. If you don't know the person very well, you could apply all three but it only takes a very brief conversation to establish what they prefer and adults can tell you, if you ask, how they prefer to receive instructions.

Children love to be trusted to do jobs and to look after aspects of their everyday life, such as putting on their own coat, preparing their cereal, buttering their toast and so on. Adults, too, respond well to being trusted and relish the challenge and the opportunity to show their skills. They are flattered to be asked. Even if the task is not done quite as you expected, remember to apply one of the core NLP principles and note their *good intention*.

There are lots of reasons why we don't delegate as much as would make our lives easier, whether to children or to adults. Which of these apply to you?

▶ I can do it better myself.
▶ I can do it quicker myself.
▶ It takes too long to explain.
▶ They might get it wrong.
▶ If they do it then I will feel I'm not needed.

Let's take a closer look at some of these statements.

'**I can do it better myself**' – you probably can, but in what way would it be better, how are you defining 'better'? Sometimes by letting someone else do something you normally do yourself you find out a better way because they approach the task differently. As long as the job's done then does it matter if it's done differently?

Insight

My husband Edward was looking after our toddler son while I returned to full-time work. When I left copious instructions on what had to be done, when and in what way, he felt completely undermined. Not only did he have no work status, but his status as father was now being questioned. He rebelled and instead of taking Paul to mother and toddler groups and Tumbletots as instructed, he took Paul out for long walks in the woods, climbing trees and walking along logs, getting dirty! I was cross because I wanted Paul's activities to continue and for his father to do the same as I had done. Then a friend of ours reminded me that I had delegated the task of entertaining our son and could not specify how that was done so long as he was safe and happily occupied. Edward interpreted the task and it was not done the same way, arguably it was better but it took a long time to accept this as I was trying to over-control out of guilt that I was not the main carer any more.

'**I can do it quicker myself**' – probably, but how important is it to have things done quickly in the long run. Children can put on Velcro shoes quicker than laced shoes, but they are not going to spend their life in Velcro shoes. Homework is done quicker if we help them, but that will not help them to learn and will undermine their confidence. Toddlers will eat quicker if we feed them, but that doesn't teach them the skills they need in life, nor does it exercise their motor skills ready for writing. Sometimes slow is better in the long run.

'It takes too long to explain' – it won't take very long to explain if you concentrate on communicating the key facts using the preferred style of the other person. You don't need irrelevant detail about *how* the task should be executed but trust that they can do this once they know *what* needs to be done.

'They might get it wrong' – but what is right? Do we mean that only our way is right? There are lots of ways of doing a task and their way may be different but not necessarily wrong. Remember the NLP term, embedded commands. This means that when we ask someone to *not* do something, we subconsciously instruct them to get it wrong or make a mistake. An example of this is 'Don't forget to test the temperature of the bath water.' You can't 'not forget' but you can 'remember'. Keep instructions in the positive. 'Don't let him near the fire' becomes 'Keep him away from the fire.'

'If they do it then I will feel I'm not needed' – why do you want to feel needed as a servant to do everything for your child? Wouldn't you rather do the things that you really *want* to do with them?

> Some things can and should be delegated, whereas other things you can make time for, now that you have delegated the others.

What to delegate then? Go back to the list you made on pp. 82–3 to remind yourself of the tasks you decided to do, dump or delegate.

Trusting each other, your child and other adults is far more difficult than we imagine, so we tend to try to do everything ourselves. This avoids confronting our fears of not being needed, or the risk of trusting someone and being let down, so instead we compensate by over-controlling. This is not a nurturing behaviour but in its way it is quite destructive, as we are not allowing our children to learn and develop self-regulation, self-preservation and self-determination. As for how it affects the adults around us, you have only to think about how *you* feel when someone doesn't trust you to do something to know just how undermining that is to your self-esteem. So let's all try to delegate more!

Part two

Applying NLP at home

5

....

Lack of confidence

In this chapter you will learn:
- *how to be confident and overcome your fears*
- *about your strengths and skills and how to use them*
- *how to cope with criticism and feelings of failure*
- *to be confident at school, sport and with friends*
- *to pass these skills on to your children*

No matter how confident we may feel in some situations, there can be other situations that we feel less able to cope with. For some it may be social situations, for others it could be conflict, or having to make a presentation, seeing their doctor or their child's teacher. The thing to remember is that you are not lacking in confidence all of the time.

We have the resource for confidence, we just need to access it. We'll do that right now. You can teach it to your children; they will enjoy it.

Circle of excellence

1 Draw a large circle on a piece of paper, or use a mat if that's easier. It needs to be large enough to step into. Let's call it the circle of excellence.
2 Think about a time when you *did* feel confident. It doesn't matter when that was or what you were doing, as long as you were confident.
3 Step into your circle of excellence and picture yourself doing that thing you do with confidence. If you are visual, give it colour and lighting as if you are in a Hollywood movie. If you are auditory you may want to give it sound and music. Really associate with the experience as if you are doing that thing right now.

(Contd)

> 4 Step out of the circle and break the state.
> 5 Repeat the process and anchor it.
> 6 Repeat steps 4 and 5 until you can trigger the feeling of confidence easily using your anchor.

Now you have accessed this confidence resource let's try it out with some situations when you may need it.

Coping with feelings of failure

According to NLP there is no failure, only feedback. Yet, as humans, we do feel low and as if we've failed at times. Sometimes it can be so bad we just want to disappear under a rock and hide until the feelings dissipate.

We do have the resources though to deal with failure and learn from feedback. Imagine if we didn't we'd still be crawling. As babies we just kept on practising until we could walk. This continues throughout childhood as we learn to read and write, ride a bike and so on. We encourage our children to overcome disappointments or failures because we know they'll get there in the end and just need our help and feedback to succeed. They don't sit around thinking and feeling a failure, they just pick themselves up and practise until at last they take their first step or use the potty.

Just as children learn from their mistakes so can we if we get in touch with the 'child' within us. As adults we need to tune into the learning experience and learn from the mistake. This is feedback.

Insight

Apparently when Thomas Edison was asked how he had coped with his failure in the 9,999 attempts to invent the light bulb, he responded that the feedback and outcome of each attempt was recorded then adjusted or changed for the next attempt until he achieved the desired outcome on the 10,000th attempt. He said he had found 9,999 ways that it did not work, which was his feedback. What he did not say was that he had *failed* 9,999 times. I'm not suggesting that we have this stoicism as parents, but the point is that if you can reframe your attempt in a positive way such that you can absorb the feedback and use it to improve next time, you will get there.

Here are some tips to avoid feelings of failure:

▶ Instead of dwelling on the negative experience, think back over what happened and why it happened.

- Consider what your internal state was at the time. Were you feeling tired or stressed?
- Use the anchoring technique (p. 21) to get yourself into a more positive state before tackling this sort of situation again.

Being aware of your 'state' will enable you to read your body by checking out how you are standing or sitting, whether you are stiff and tense, whether your breathing is easy and relaxed or short and shallow. How are your shoulders – hunched, drooping forwards in a defensive way or just nicely relaxed? If you feel that your body is holding in your stress and not allowing you to feel relaxed there are lots of things you can do to alleviate that.

Have a go

Tense and relax the stiff areas a few times and be aware of how they feel now.

Go for a walk to loosen up. Exercise is a great releaser of stress and tension so if you notice that this is how you feel most of the time then introduce some cycling or running into the day, especially in advance of times of the day when you notice this feeling of failure most often.

Look up! It's hard to feel down or a failure if you look up. Looking down encourages introspection and reflection. If you look up, you can access your memory of when you get it right and you can visualize what it looks like to succeed. If your child is feeling a failure say 'Look up' and then start talking about what happened.

Visual – Imagine a lovely relaxed place you'd rather be in. Focus on the colours and the shapes and make it into a 'film' with you as the main star. See yourself in this gorgeous place and imagine the clothes you'd be wearing, how your hair and face look and what shoes and bag you have. You are the film director; make the film just as amazing as you want – no budget limitations!

Auditory – Play your favourite piece of music in your head. Be the conductor and bring in every musical instrument in the orchestra or band and play them as loudly as you want. Are there other sounds you'd like to hear? Bring them in too. Imagine you are playing one of the instruments, which will it be? Play it

(Contd)

loudly and then softer, enjoying the excellence of the tones and melody.

Kinaesthetic – You respond well to movement and action so the idea of a walk might well appeal to you. Check whether you are too hot or too cold, are you feeling comfortable? How are you feeling, be aware of your body and if you can, move about, laugh at a remembered joke or something your child did recently.

Control your state at stressful times and put yourself in a more resourceful state, then you will be able to access feedback.

FEEDBACK

When we communicate with people, we receive a response – this is our *feedback*. We are communicating all the time by how we stand, where we stand within our environment, how we arrange our environment, the words we use and our facial expressions.

You can tell from a person's response what was understood from your communication or the action you took. If the response was not as you intended, follow up with a request for feedback. There are lots of ways of doing this, for example:

> *'Sorry, what did I say?'*
> *'I'm not sure that came across as I intended.'*
> *'Let's try again.'*

This may seem awkward the first time you do it, but I'm sure you'll agree that it's preferable to wondering what went wrong. What's the worst that can happen? Is that worse than feeling a failure?

You can also help your children by giving them feedback. For example:

> *'I don't know whether you meant to look/sound/come across so aggressively, so perhaps you'd like to have another go.'*

What if your sense of failure is a belief you hold from your past? Has someone in your childhood said or done something that has left you with the fear of failure? This is what NLP calls a limiting belief and you can *choose* whether to hold this belief or not. If the feelings are preventing you from achieving what you want to achieve or from being a happy parent then you may want to revisit these beliefs.

Insight

I had a limiting belief about conflict. My parents didn't like arguments so they bottled up their feelings and expected us to do the same. Arguing was unacceptable and scary. Then I went to university and slowly learned how to argue safely and respectfully, but I still had a problem doing this with people I was close to. My usual response was to exit the room and cry. My husband found this infuriating. The belief that arguing with a loved one was scary held me back from having an adult relationship. I chose to discard this old childish belief and take on the belief that arguing can deepen an adult relationship if done with respect.

Some limiting beliefs that lead to feelings of failure belong in our past and need to be revisited as adults to check whether they are outdated. After all, we have changed since childhood, learned more about ourselves, grown up and developed new skills that make those limiting beliefs no longer true for us.

Sara believed that she was not clever enough to go to university because her mother had left school at 15 and none of her siblings had stayed on at school. When, at 40, she started to ask herself why she had no qualifications and considered doing some evening classes, her mother questioned the sense in doing any learning at her age. It took a huge amount of faith in herself and her abilities to overcome this limiting belief. But now she has signed up and is eager to start. The word 'can't' has been replaced now by 'But what if I can?' and she's moved on from her childhood beliefs.

When we feel those first self-doubts creeping in, those destructive and limiting beliefs that we are not capable of doing something, or a feeling that we have failed at something, we have the resources to silence them. Remind yourself of your skills. Remind yourself to use the feedback and your response to the situation as a resource to move forward. Then draw on the skills you have, perhaps in another area of your life, and apply them to where you most need them.

From time to time we feel we have failed as a parent, partner, lover, daughter or friend. This is natural; after all, we are not perfect. How do you think you have failed? What can you do to succeed? It is in your power. You can turn the situation around by asking yourself:

> *'What would success in that context look/sound/feel like?'*
> *'What skills do I need to achieve this desired outcome?'*
> *'Where else do I currently use that skill?'*

'How can I bring it across into the area of my life where I need it now?'

Tip

When you feel a sense of failure, it's good to use the anchoring technique to put yourself in a resourceful state so you can access your transferable skills.

Do a quick audit of your general skills. This is a great help when you feel you've failed at something. What are you good at? Write your list here.

I am good at:

1

2

3

4

5

6

7

8

9

10

Now add in what others say about you because they see you in a different light. Perhaps you are self-critical and don't always see your assets or they are so familiar to you that you take them for granted.

My friends and family say I am good at:

1

2

3

4

5

6

7

8

9

10

Now revisit those areas where you feel you've failed and look back at these two lists. Which of these skills can you take from a different context and work with?

Where I feel I have failed:

A skill I have that will help in this situation:

What could I do differently by using this skill in the area I want to change?

I can:

Do it and ask for feedback.

This exercise is very useful with children too, of course.

Paul finds reading very hard and he gives up easily when he gets to a difficult or unfamiliar word. 'I can't do it,' he groans, and closes the book. Paul is very good at sport and plays quite aggressively; he tackles and perseveres until he gets the ball off the opposition.

'What makes you good at football, Paul?'

'Because I like it.'

'Don't you like reading?'

'No.'

'Why not?'

'Because I can't do it.'

'So why can you do football and not reading?'

'Because I am fast and because I am not scared of trying to get the ball.'

'Are you scared of reading?'

'Yes, because I keep getting it wrong.'

'If that difficult word was a ball, you would keep trying until you got it wouldn't you?'

'Yes.'

'Shall we pretend that each difficult word is a ball and that because you are fast and not scared you can work it out?'

Children are very good at imagining things and they use metaphors quite naturally, so it wasn't hard for Paul to pretend each word he didn't recognize was a ball. By applying his fast and 'not scared' skills from football, he approached his reading quite differently, speeded up and was soon reading confidently on his own.

You can use clean language skills to reduce the sense of failure your child will experience. Expressions such as:

▶ 'Try to…' suggest failure
▶ 'Do you think you can…' imply there is a possibility that they can't
▶ 'But don't…' is an embedded command for them to do the opposite
▶ 'Anyone can…' is a distortion by way of generalizing, and is not true.

Freeing your child to succeed by not limiting their self-belief is arguably one of the most wonderful gifts you can give your child.

Not being a 'good mother'

This statement, in NLP terms, is externally referenced and shows that we judge ourselves as we think others judge us; our reference point for our behaviour is outside of us. That could mean your own mother or grandmother, your partner or children, other mums or friends. Perhaps those with a faith may judge themselves by the dictates of their religion.

If we were internally referenced we would judge ourselves by our *own* moral and behavioural code, which makes a lot more sense even if it may seem an impossible switch to make.

The problem with the notion of being a 'good mother' is that attitudes towards mothering have changed over time; our own mothers relied on what their mothers believed and so on.

Fran's mother did not work but looked after her children, made sure a hot meal was on the table when her husband arrived home, cleaned the house, repaired clothes and tended the garden. Fran knew she could not afford to do this like her own mother because she and her husband needed two salaries. She still tried, though, to do as much as she could of what constituted, for her, being a 'good mother'. She would come home after a busy day at work to play with the children, cook a meal and put them to bed. No matter what she did she still felt a failure as a mother, although most of us today would say she was a great success!

In the nineteenth century, a good mother raised her children to have strong moral codes, skills such as embroidery and playing the piano, and concentrated on making good marriages for them. You can see this in works by Jane Austen and Alcott's *Little Women*. The first half of the twentieth century saw two world wars, with mothers sacrificing their sons to the battlefields and daughters being trained to take their place in factories and schools. The second half of the century offered huge changes for women in education and the workplace with unprecedented career opportunities. This in turn led to the situation we find ourselves in today where women are as educated as men and have been led to expect interesting well-paid jobs, but actually find in reality that the sacrifice in terms of family life is huge and often too great.

We have seen the rise and fall of the 'have it all' generation and are now seeing, as a result, the burgeoning self-employment and small business opportunities which allow women to work flexibly and juggle career and childcare more easily.

Juggling is not easy. Whether we are juggling a full-time job, part-time job, self-employment, several children, even an elderly relative perhaps, we give ourselves almost impossible standards to live up to, and 'fail' at. Setting achievable, manageable and controllable goals is an important step in countering those feelings of failure.

Make sure you are '**outcome thinking**' not '**problem thinking**'. The difference is enormous. Problem thinking is focusing on the problem you think needs solving, for example, 'I can't even cover the cost of childcare with the job I'm in now, what can I do? I will have to quit.' Outcome thinking focuses on the solution, for example, 'How do I get a job that pays enough to cover the costs of childcare?' Focus on what you want for yourself, *not* what others want for you or what will gain you approval from others, but what *you* want and what fulfils your own values as a mother in today's environment. Phrase the goals as towards goals not away-from.

Outcome thinking

1 Find a quiet time and place and close your eyes. Imagine you are going to sleep with all the problems you feel you have at the moment.
2 During the sleep, something magical happens to take away all those problems and negative feelings.
3 Wake up and they will all be gone.
4 Take some time to notice what is different now. How is everything better now? What is working that wasn't working for you before?

This exercise will clarify what your outcomes are, and what areas of your life you want to address.

You can use a time line to work on this further.

Placing outcomes on your time line

1 Stay in that zone where the dream has come true, the magic has worked and you are in that positive place where your outcomes have been achieved.
2 Now imagine a line in front of you representing time. The line goes from today through to the future.
3 Stand on the line at the point where your outcomes have been met. Clearly imagine what it looks, sounds and feels like for you. What can you see, what can you hear and what are you feeling right now? The more clearly you can imagine this desired state, the more you will act as if it is true for you now. How does this new 'you' fit with your values and beliefs?
4 Now step back to a point that represents today. Can you see more clearly what you want to do to achieve your outcome and what this means to you in terms of being 'a good mother'. What has been your pay-off for holding on to your current way of behaving? Can you think of how you could still get that pay-off by a different method?

However you feel about yourself, NLP thinking is that there is no failure, only feedback, so if what you're doing now is not working, then change what you're doing because 'if you always do what you've always done, you will always get what you've always got'. The thing that has to change is your behaviour. Use feedback from what you are doing to help you internally reference – to use your own beliefs and values to judge your own behaviour.

Your *own* values are important, not what others expect of you. If you can model someone whom you think is 'a good mother', then this is a useful tool. Who for you is a model of excellence as a 'good mother'? Make it a project and observe them. Talk to them about how they do what they do and, crucially, what their beliefs are about being a 'good mother'. Can you take on those beliefs, and, if you do, do they work for you too?

> Lots of new mums find renewed love and admiration for their own mother, now they appreciate what she did for them. This could be a good time to get closer to your mum and model her.

The feeling that you are not a good mother is one that you have *chosen* to have; it is not forced upon you by others. *You* have chosen this on the basis of external references such as the expectations and approval of others. You have the choice to give yourself approval, be internally referenced, adopt outcome thinking and change behaviours to become more the sort of mother you want to be... for yourself.

Embarrassment

Do you sometimes find yourself cringing with embarrassment because of something your child just said or did, or perhaps something that you said or did? It's easy to do that when you are tired and stressed. Maybe you find yourself losing concentration, forgetting someone's name or worse. Normally you can just laugh it off, but sometimes this just doesn't work and you feel embarrassed and stupid. This can lead to low self-esteem and sometimes even a fear of socializing because you are worried the same thing will happen again.

Here are some practical solutions:

▶ Ask a close friend or your partner to come with you to any important meetings at school, with the doctor or solicitor.

They can make notes for you and remind you of the questions you wanted to ask.

▶ Talk through with a colleague what you want to say to your boss and make notes as an *aide memoire* for the meeting.

▶ Use sticky notes or reminders, lists and so on.

You are not superwoman and you can't be expected to function on small bouts of disturbed sleep.

It is helpful to use the NLP logical levels (p. 25) to help, and it works just as well for children's embarrassing situations such as bed-wetting or nervous tics.

Firstly think about the *environment*. What aspects of your environment trigger feelings of embarrassment?

Sarah used to get embarrassed going to the doctor with her baby because she tended to fear the worst. She would worry so much that she forgot what the doctor said almost as soon as he'd said it, so she had to ask him to repeat it, which made her feel stupid. She was too embarrassed to ask a friend, so I suggested she research the baby's symptoms on the internet so then she'd have an idea of what to ask the doctor and she'd be more likely to understand his answers. This solution worked in two ways. She found that the information on the internet reassured her that her baby was normal and gave practical solutions she could try without having to go to the doctor at all. When she did have to visit the doctor, she knew what the possibilities were and they had a more adult-to-adult conversation, which quickly concluded with an agreement on how to treat the problem. When I asked Sarah how she understood the doctor now but didn't before, she said that knowing more about the problem put her more on a level footing where she felt more confident and alert and able to concentrate better on his words rather than on her worrying about the baby.

Think about how to get take back control in a situation and you will find this helps enormously.

Children can do this too. If there's something they are embarrassed about, discuss it with them and list all the possible ways they can get control of the situation. Don't dismiss any ideas that either of you have, write them all down. Then go through the list deciding which ones might work and dismissing those that definitely won't. Agree which you will try first, and reward success with a reminder that your child has control. Manage their expectations, however, because children generally have less control over their environment, and you can't control an environment where you can't be, such as school or in a friend's home.

> Patterns of behaviour that cause embarrassment can result in real social phobias.

Modelling can also be a useful tool in these situations.

Insight

My brother Andy is fantastic socially. I watched him and noticed that he seemed to think for a second before approaching someone. What was he thinking in those seconds? I asked him.

He explained that he observed as much as he could about the person and then decided on a good question that would 'break the ice'. He said with women he would pick on something they were wearing and say something like 'Those are amazing shoes, where did you get them?' or 'That colour reminds me of my holiday' – something that would easily get a conversation flowing. With men, he would ask them about a recent football match or other sporting event. Other tactics were to 'share a secret' such as admitting he didn't know the name of a food on the buffet table. This tactic also meant that they would have to move together to the buffet table, which avoids being rooted to the spot in embarrassment.

I asked him about the moments before he walks into a social situation. He said he anchors a good feeling about a party he went to when everything worked well, and says to himself before he goes in, 'I'm going to have a great time here.' He would also make a point of saying goodbye to each person he'd had a good conversation with and thanking them for making the party so enjoyable for him. This meant that he left with a good feeling he could anchor for the next one. I modelled his behaviour and it really helped me overcome my embarrassment in social situations.

What skills do you have for overcoming embarrassment? Remember, fundamental to NLP philosophy is that you have all the resources you need and can model those you want to acquire. Can you think of an occasion when you were confident and self-assured? Think about that time and how it felt, then anchor a feeling of calm and self-control and use it in situations when you could feel embarrassed.

> **Note:** If you enjoyed the circle of excellence exercise you can use that one instead.

Think about your beliefs and values; these influence your behaviour. Do you have a belief that is limiting you? Do you go into a potentially embarrassing situation believing you will be embarrassed?

Another way of tackling a limiting belief is to act 'as if'. This is great for children who love to play make believe. Decide you will act as if you have all the confidence in the world, feel calm and in control.

Auditory – Repeat these words to yourself: 'I am calm, I am in control. I am confident.'

Visual – Practise in the mirror looking confident, check your body posture, make eye contact and give the impression of someone who is super calm.

Kinaesthetic – You may want to have actions that make you feel confident like pulling your shoulders back or hugging yourself before entering a potential embarrassing situation.

If the situation is one involving your child, you could act 'as if' your child is really good and well behaved, even in supermarkets! If you act as if you have a fantastic child, they do seem to behave better as if they have to live up to this. Remember, even if you have images in your mind of embarrassing situations, they aren't always embarrassing are they? We tend to remember the excruciating ones, but this is generalized thinking – 'always playing up', 'never behaving', 'always embarrass me' are not really true. Work with the happy memories when they have not been embarrassing and act 'as if' that is the norm. If we change our way of thinking, our behaviour, and theirs, changes too.

What if you identify with being an embarrassed person most of the time? Are you saying to yourself, 'I am embarrassed' as if it is your identity? Replace the 'I am embarrassed' with 'I feel embarrassed when…', then work with the beliefs and behaviours, using anchors and reducing the limiting beliefs. Take advantage of modelling where you can and remember you have the resource not to feel this way, so find where it is in your experiences and regain it for your role as a mum or dad.

Envy

There are many reasons nowadays why we might envy others. We might envy their job, their children, their house, car, designer clothes, partner, holidays, appearance and so on. We've all felt it at some time or other and it isn't a good feeling is it?

The interesting thing about envy is that while we are aware of how we envy others, we often miss the fact that they envy us. We may be quite surprised to discover that we have something that others envy.

Switch to becoming internally rather than externally focused.

Visualization exercise

Think of a person who has a quality you envy in them. Paint a picture in your mind exaggerating the aspect about which you feel envy. If it's their car, for example, make it bright and shiny, your favourite colour and see the person going on a fantastic journey somewhere you want to go. If it's their house, picture them in it with the house looking as if it is in the pages of a glossy magazine. What I want you to do is *acknowledge* the envy and welcome it in – bring it on!

Now replace them in that picture and picture *yourself* in the scene. You are driving that car, living in that house. How does it feel? What would be different for you if you had that thing you crave?

Think about you as a person, who are *you*? What values do you have? What is important to you in life? Does the thing you feel envy for fit into this picture of yourself?

The object of your envy makes a superb model. Having identified what it is you really envy about someone, use them as your model. Watch them and notice how they behave. For example, attractive people hold themselves differently; they are more erect, give better eye contact and they behave 'as if' they are attractive, which for you, they are. Now *you* do that! Dress, walk and talk 'as if' you were the most beautiful person in the room. Let the clothes you choose in the morning matter. Even if you can't afford a designer wardrobe, you feel depressed, or are six months pregnant, dress to impress. You will feel so much more confident and look more attractive.

Sometimes when we feel envious of others it is because we may be suffering from low self-esteem. It may seem to us that someone else is better than we are, more successful and more aligned to their goals in life. If you believe this to be true, now may be a good time to revisit your goals. What do you want in life, who and how do you want to be? What are your values? What are those qualities that make you who you are?

Who inspires you? Think about a personality, a politician or world leader, celebrity or whoever you find really inspirational, and look up to as a model for who you want to be. Does this person have qualities that you admire? In what way do you have these qualities? If you recognize these qualities in others you already have them.

How do you inspire others? You do, you know! Think about how you inspire others. What qualities do you have that others admire in you? Write these down.

I inspire others in the way I:

We each have unique gifts and rather than compare yourself with someone else who you think has something you want, consider modelling their skills and adding these to your own to enrich your own self-esteem rather than wanting to actually *be* them.

Children sometimes appear to envy what their friends have, how late they are allowed to stay up, where they go on holiday and so on. Hearing about this can get us down when we are doing our best. Acknowledge the emotion – 'It seems that you are envious of what Ollie has' – rather than give them a list of all the reasons they should be grateful for what they have, tempting though that might be! Get them to do some **perceptual positioning** – 'Is there anything you have that Ollie may be envious of?' Putting themselves in their friend's position helps them to see that we all have different things, no one has everything. That includes toys and games, sports prowess, reading ability and so on. If it is a *skill* they are envious of, show them how to model this and how to take the skill into their own life.

Instead of viewing envy as a negative, destructive emotion, see it as feedback rather than failure. What is this emotion telling you? The positive aspect of envy is that it shows you skills you can model and it can act as a check-in with your own sense of alignment with your values and goals in life. That new sports car may be your friend's metaphor for success but perhaps that isn't yours, so refocus on what is important to you and your identity and acknowledge that you are *you* and not them.

Knowing your strengths

Maybe you've been asked this question when applying for a new job and you have to fill in an application form. You need to know your own strengths.

It isn't the easiest thing to do because we tend to take our own strengths for granted. Perhaps we have been doing what we do for as long as we can remember and the behaviour is so natural that we aren't even aware of it.

Insight

My friend Helen is fantastic at achieving rapport. She makes excellent eye contact, physically stands very close, even nudging me with her elbow as she talks. She pays attention to what I say to her and uses the same words in her responses, along with lively facial and hand movements to show her involvement. Her daughter Tiffany does exactly the same and isn't even aware she has this skill because she's probably been modelling her mum since she was born.

Friends often have the same qualities as us, which is why we are attracted to them. Ask yourself where and how you have this strength you've observed in someone else.

1 Here is a list of qualities. Tick all those that your friends or acquaintances might observe in you.

Attractive	Sporty
Patient	Observant
Kind	Respectful
Listens well	Approachable
Artistic	Well organized
Good driver	Energetic
Punctual	Considerate
Smart	Focused
Funny	Honest
Creative	Team player
Clever	

2 Add to this list any others that could describe you.

3 Now look at the words opposite and circle those that define you and are what is important about who you are. It might be easier to think of it another way. If someone were to say you were 'not very [chosen word]' how would you feel? Sometimes thinking about the opposite helps us focus on what is important to us.

4 Look at the words you have circled as being important strengths to you. Think about *why* they are important – what are the underlying values you hold that support those strengths? What do those values say about you?

5 Now look at the strengths you have *not* circled and think about why those are less important and what that says about you. Remember to be 'disassociated' because you may not notice what others notice.

If you're doing this exercise with your child or teenager, you may have to help them to disassociate by reminding them of situations where you have observed that strength in them.

Once you have a list of strengths that define you as an altogether loveable person, you can take this exercise to another level to understand how these strengths can help you to be a happier parent.

You may have some issues around parenting that you would like to address, maybe something you'd like to find easier to do such as 'finding time for myself' or 'having some energy'. Whatever it is, write down what you want to access these strengths for.

I want to access my strengths so I can:

Look at that list of strengths and think about which of these will be most useful to you in the task you've set. Be creative about how you can use the strength to address the issue.

Insight

I am punctual. What this means is that I arrive wherever I need to be about 15 minutes early. I use this time to email my friends, organize my social life, read for pleasure, write notes for my next chapter, tidy the car, shop online and so on. I have used one strength, 'being punctual', to address an issue I had about not having any time for 'my stuff' after work.

See your strengths as a portable toolbox, a resource to tackle whatever you have to do. Explore them further by asking 'What does this mean I can do?' and move on to look at how you can use it in a bigger context to address an issue that's bothering you.

If you ask your partner to do the exercises as well, you could have double the resource because you might agree that some tasks are best done by the other. If you can do this then you can add 'ability to delegate' to your list of accessible strengths!

Similarly, work with your children to produce a list of their strengths and you may find that they have a strength you hadn't appreciated and can access in order to free up your own time.

> **Insight**
> When I did this exercise with one of my daughters, I realized she has the ability to focus without being distracted and that made her much more efficient at cooking the supper because she didn't get sidetracked by other tasks as I did. So I delegated and this pleased her enormously as it meant she could decide what to cook.

This is an excellent exercise to help children focus on their strengths, and how they can use them. Encourage your children to think of the strengths of their siblings too, which is great for bonding and self-esteem.

Coping with criticism

There are two types of criticism, overt and covert, and either can knock us back. Overt criticism is when someone specifically says something critical about you to your face; covert is when you think someone is being critical of you even though they haven't actively said anything. This can happen quite frequently when out with your children.

> **Insight**
> My nine-year-old loves to weigh the fruit and veg and print off the price ticket on one of those machines in the supermarket. To be honest I've found this a great way to keep his interest when I'm shopping and more or less guarantees he will eat the veg. The other day a woman was 'tut-tutting' as he was using the machine and then told me off – 'He shouldn't be playing with the machine you know.' I was furious because he was using it in just the same way she would, and I thought she was completely out of order. Nevertheless I still took it as a criticism of his behaviour and mine for allowing it.

The part of us that accepts the criticism, even when it is unfair, is our inner critical Parent telling us off. We need to move into Adult mode and fast! Weigh up quickly whether the overt or covert criticism is justified. Would someone else viewing the situation, an impartial witness, consider that you or your child had done something wrong? Disassociate yourself and your child and you won't take it so personally. If you don't think another passing customer would be critical then accept that this critical person is being unreasonable and perhaps has had a bad day, has a headache or is tired. For some reason that has nothing to do with you, they are unhappy and you just happen to be in the wrong place at the wrong time. You don't have to retaliate or respond to the criticism.

If, in Adult mode, you decide that they do have a point, then you can do the adult thing and apologize, accept the feedback and either point out to your child what they have done or, better still, show them how to do it better.

Some people get a pay-off from criticizing others because it makes them feel powerful. Decide for *yourself* whether you are in the wrong by applying your own values, not theirs. Use internal referencing to consider what they are saying as feedback that you can either choose to take on board and learn from, or reject if you don't think it reasonable.

You will find criticism harder to take than someone who is internally referenced, who will judge themselves by their own internal values and beliefs and be less affected by the views of others. So how do you switch from being externally referenced to being internally referenced?

NLP has a great technique for helping us replace an unwanted thought or negative reaction with a more resourceful one. If you find yourself in a situation where you would usually respond badly to criticism, you can replace it with a different reaction.

Swishing exercise

1 Decide how you want to respond instead and decide on a replacement feeling. Imagine yourself having that feeling and keep disassociated as if watching yourself from afar. Make the image really attractive to you and compelling.

2 Think about what triggers the usual unwanted response. What happens just before you respond with the feeling you want

(Contd)

to avoid? It could be a word, an expression, a smell even. Associate into that trigger. Make it centre stage in your mind.

3 Now in the bottom corner of that image put your preferred replacement image. Imagine it like a postage stamp in the corner of your unwanted image.

4 Now 'swish'. Switch the small one to the centre to replace the unwanted image. You can say 'swish' as you do that.

Children enjoy this one. You can use it with vegetables or foods they don't like. You may need to do it a few times, slowly at first, then speed up. After a while you'll get so good at this you can do it in seconds.

If you are pretty good at acting, then act 'as if' you are calm, controlled and fair-minded and when you are next in a situation where you feel criticized, remember to act this same way.

Feedback is extremely important because it is the information you need to change your behaviour. If your behaviour, or your child's, prompts negative feedback, you have to disassociate and internally reference to decide if someone witnessing the behaviour would also have given negative feedback, in which case you need to change the behaviour. If, having disassociated, you decide that the person giving negative feedback was simply having a bad day, or that your behaviour was perfectly reasonable according to your values and beliefs, then you can stop feeling bad about the criticism.

When someone gives you feedback that you would in the past have considered to be 'criticism', look on it as a gift and thank them. First, bridge the gap. Reflect for a moment and decide whether their feedback is fair and reasonable from what they have seen and heard and felt. If it is fair, then just accept it and next time you are in that situation try a different approach.

If you think that their feedback is unfair, think again because what you think you said or did or meant is actually of no importance. What matters, the nature of the communication, is what the other person perceives or thinks you meant. We've all been in a situation where someone says something and we have taken it as a criticism because we may suspect that deep down there is some truth in it. Their intention may not have been to be rude or unkind. It's more helpful to assume that behind every communication is a good intention and that good intention is to give feedback.

Think about how to give good feedback to your child. How do you like to receive feedback? Have you heard of 'sandwich feedback'? That works really well for children. First, say something you liked about what they did. Then say what you didn't like (that's the meat in the sandwich), then summarize with another positive point. Here's an example:

> *'Paul, it was really sweet of you to collect the eggs for me and show them to Jack (acknowledge the good intention). Did you realize though that you didn't replace the door and one of the hens got out (feedback)? You must be more careful (criticism) because the fox could get her and that would be very sad. Next time you want to be helpful (positive), please remember the door.'*

Regardless of what you meant to communicate, what the recipient understands by it is, in effect, what was said. This means that you have to be really careful to communicate what you want your child to take from it. How many times have we, as adults, been hurt by a chance remark that happened to hit a raw spot? Sometimes it isn't so much the words used but the tone and emphasis that we are hurt by.

Coping with criticism is all about identifying the *positive intention* to give *feedback* then *disassociating* so you can decide whether you agree when you *internally reference*.

When criticizing children, express it as what you observe rather than making assumptions about their motives. Assume a positive intention and use the 'sandwich' technique to show how to move forward. It's also helpful to show them where they have the resource to behave differently next time.

Giving your child confidence

Even children who seem confident in certain parts of their life can lack confidence in other areas. It is not unusual for a child who is very confident at home to feel overwhelmed at school, and a child who is confident among friends to become very shy with those they don't know. The skill as a parent is in teaching them how to access the confident feelings they have in one place or situation and apply this confidence elsewhere.

One way of doing this, which works well with children, is to make-believe and suggest they pretend they are confident or act 'as if' they are confident. You can do this at home first. Ask them to imagine they are in the situation where they feel confident and brave. Perhaps this is when they have a friend round to play. They can even dress up for this. Perhaps they have favourite clothes that make them feel confident, or they feel more confident if they are a character from Star Wars or one of the video games they play. You can pick one of their favourite characters and say 'How would this character be when they are confident?' Once they have the confident feeling, ask them to anchor it (see p. 21). They can then use this anchor in situations they find more difficult.

One reason why children don't always feel confident is that they compare themselves with other children, usually those who are better at something than them. In our schools these days, competition is a dirty word, but however much the school may try to rule it out, children naturally compete and will continue to do so as adults – it's a natural tendency.

Encourage them to compare themselves instead with how they were last month or last term, so they can see how much they have improved in something.

Show your child how to be internally referenced rather than externally referenced as this will give them a useful skill in life. So if your child usually gets eight out of ten for his spelling test and this week gets nine, then he should be justly proud of himself and not compare himself with those who regularly get ten out of ten. An externally referenced child will constantly compare to others and not notice their own improvements.

If children want to improve and gain self-confidence from being better at something, they can model the person they want to learn from. This external reference is a source from where they can learn to be better themselves rather than seeing the comparison in a negative light. Following on from the example above of the child who got nine out of ten in his spelling and wanted to get ten, if he were to find out what strategy the ten out of ten child used and copy it, he would soon improve his score. More on that in a later chapter about how children learn.

Children are inclined to use generalizations and distortions such as 'Everyone is better than me'. Ask them, 'Who, exactly?' and 'How are they better?' to encourage them to see the situation more realistically. 'I always get low marks' may just mean that they were disappointed with a recent mark. By noticing when they got a good mark, they may start to see a pattern. Perhaps they revised for that particular test.

Another way to switch their negative self-talk to a more upbeat, positive and confident orientation is to notice whether they talk about what they *want* or what they *don't want*. Do they work hard so they *don't* get into trouble or do they work hard so they *do* get good marks? Working 'towards' rather than 'away from' things tends to result in a more confident approach.

Even young children can lack confidence before they start school because they are shy or find it difficult to make friends easily. Show them the skills they need by modelling them – for example, go up to someone with your child, someone *you* don't know and show them how to start a conversation.

Have a go

1 Ask your child who they most admire at school. Ask who they think is the most popular, prettiest, sportiest, or whatever they value in other children that they would like to have.

2 When they say the name, ask them to describe what they admire in that child. Ask them how they are like that child, because we tend to notice character and personality traits in others that we also have ourselves.

3 Then ask them what other children admire in them. It can be an inspirational experience when they realize that they have something others want.

4 Ask your child to list what they are good at, anything at all. It could just be something they consider trivial like knowing the words of a song or being able to skip with a rope. Whatever they say, show them how being good at that thing also means they are good at other related things. For example:

'What are you good at?'

(Contd)

'Well, I know all the words of the latest Leona Lewis song.'

'You know all the words of the latest Leona Lewis song? How do you do that?'

'I listen very hard lots of times and sing it through until I know the words.'

'That's great! So you are good at listening well, you have a good memory and can replay what you know. How could you use that skill to learn your times tables?'

'I could make up a song for my times tables because I always get them wrong.'

'You *always* get them wrong?'

'Well I get them wrong when I write them down, but I get them right when I say the answer.'

This child probably has an auditory preference and by knowing this they can translate what they learn into their preference for easier learning and remembering.

Helping your child to understand how they learn and what they are good at gives them confidence that they can apply to other things, whatever age they are. It works for you too!

Supporting schoolwork

Many of us worry about how much to help our children and how to help them. We settle somewhere on a scale between actually doing the homework for them and leaving everything to the school. At different times in their school life they will need more help, and other times less. This section is for those times when they need a helping hand.

Let's start with a recap on how your child learns best.

Visual preference

Neat and tidy

Good at thinking ahead

Notice their surroundings

Good spellers

Speak fast

Quite well organized

Like to look good

Remember what they saw rather than heard

Memorize by visualizing

Prefer written instructions rather than being told

Prefer to read themselves rather than be read to

Answer questions briefly

Arty more than musical

Not usually bothered by noise

Good readers

Tend to doodle

Would rather be shown than told

Sometimes stumble over finding the right words

Auditory preference

Talk to themselves

Move their lips as they read

Good mimic

Tend to speak in rhythmic patterns

More musical than arty

Remember what was said rather than what was shown

Can spell better out loud than by writing it down

Easily distracted by noise

Like to read out loud

Find writing difficult

Speak well

Learn by listening

Talkative, love discussion

Kinaesthetic preference

Speak slowly

Touch people to get their attention

Physical and fidgety

Use a finger as a pointer when reading

Use action words

Have messy handwriting

Like games

Respond to physical rewards

Stand close when talking to someone

Learn by doing

Move hands while speaking

Like plot-driven books

Want to act things out

Teachers will usually use all three learning styles as a 'catch all' because they know about NLP, but as you're only working with one child at a time, you can focus on their preferred style to help them understand their schoolwork.

Here are some examples of how they work in practice.

LITERACY

Visual child

Ask them to write out the word, look carefully at it and then visualize the word written on a piece of paper. They can choose what colour to imagine it and write it themselves. It may help to link the written word with a picture of what it is. When reading, pay attention to the look of a word and work out the pattern with them.

Here is a great game for boosting your child's visual memory for spelling and mental arithmetic.

PELMANISM

Take a standard pack of 52 cards and lay them face down in straight ordered lines on the table so they form a square, about seven cards by seven cards, with the odd remaining ones down the side. It is important that players face the cards so they can see them clearly.

Now each of you take a turn to flip over two cards, one at a time. Keep them face up and move your hand away so the card can be seen clearly by both players. This is important so you can get an image of the card in you head.

If they are both the same number (they won't be the same suit unless you're using two packs) then the player keeps the cards and has another turn. Keep going until two are not the same. Now the other person has a go and again turns over two cards making sure all players can see the cards clearly. You keep the pairs you make and the winner is the player with the most pairs.

This game can also be played alone, and to make it exciting your child can time themselves to see how quickly they can pair up the pack.

KIM'S GAME

Place ten items on a tray and cover them with a tea towel. Each player needs a piece of paper and a pen. Take the cover off the tray and let the children look at the items on the tray. They may not write anything yet, of course. Give them about five minutes to look at the items, but as they get better you can reduce this time to a minute or, if they get really good, 30 seconds!

Now cover the tray again and they must write down as many of the ten items as they can remember. If you have several children playing

the game you may need to say the name of the item and let them
touch and feel them because auditory and kinaesthetic children need
this to aid their memory.

> While everyone has a preferred learning style, teachers will not always be able
> to present lessons using all three so it is useful to improve the skills in a style
> that is not your preferred style. Even if your child is auditory or kinaesthetic
> play these visual memory games with them to improve their visual memory.
>
> Apparently the best learning and memory skills are achieved when we have
> two styles used together so boosting visual memory is beneficial as so much of
> our data comes via the internet which is largely visual.

Auditory child

Sound out the letters or combinations of letters phonetically. Make
the sounds very clear and slow so they can link the sound and
the letters. It helps to learn words with similar sounds together.
Expressive reading will help so they can make a link with the sound
of the word and the word itself.

If your child is auditory then they learn by asking, hearing and
remembering the answer. They can speak more fluently than they
can read or write and enjoy discussion and arguing. To build their
auditory memory, here's a good game.

AUNTIE FLO

One person starts 'My Auntie Flo went to the market and she bought
a…', and they name a product such as a banana. The next person
continues, 'My Aunty Flo went to the market and she bought a
banana and a…', and they add another item such as a saucepan. So
it goes on until someone can no longer remember all the items. See
how long you can keep it going! A visual child playing this game will
remember the items by picturing them and probably has an image in
his head of poor Auntie Flo buried under her huge pile of shopping
by the end of the game!

GRANDMOTHER'S FOOTSTEPS

One child is blindfolded and the other children see how close they
can creep up to him without him pointing at them. The blindfolded
child is stretching his auditory muscles trying to hear every sound and
place the direction it is coming from. This game builds auditory skills.

Kinaesthetic child

Your child will learn best by physically writing out the words lots
of times and practising reading. For young children, you can buy

sandpaper letters from Montessori sources and these allow the child to feel the letters and notice the shape in preparation for reading and writing them. Shared reading seems to help a kinaesthetic child because of it being more of an activity and the physicality of sitting together.

You can also use magnetic or plastic letters for your child to trace their fingers over and make words with.

NUMERACY

Visual child

Again, ask them to write the number and then visualize what it looks like. For example, take the number three and put out three counters or blocks. Cuisenaire rods, available on Amazon, or golden beads from Montessori sources, all help children get the visual impression of numbers.

Auditory child

There are plenty of number songs and times tables chants and tunes that will help an auditory child learn numbers for mathematics work.

Kinaesthetic child

The kinesthetic child will learn best by doing. Physically playing with rods or beads, weighing ingredients for cooking or playing 'shops' will all help.

Once children know and work with their preference, they have the tools for learning and can, with your help, translate what they learn into a language they can understand.

If your child says 'I can't do it' or 'Please help me'

The best response to 'I can't do it' is 'But what if you could?' If they ask 'Please help me', you can sit down with them, get them something to eat or drink, read out the question or look at the work but silent encouragement may be enough to motivate them to do it. Asking for help could be about having some attention and it doesn't have to involve actually doing the work.

HELPING YOUR CHILD DO BETTER

There have been studies done to explore what makes the difference to children between doing well at school and just doing well enough. These studies have found that children whose parents take an active interest and reinforce the link between working hard at school and getting an interesting and well-paid job, do best at school. Children need to have goals so they know they are working towards something that they really want. It is unlikely that they will have a definite career in mind, but even if they frequently change their ideas as to what they want to do in the future, it helps to have a future goal. Ask them what they'd like to be doing or ask them whose job they'd like. Just going through the thought process of what they'd like to do helps to see the connection between schoolwork and a desirable outcome.

It is much easier for children to work when there is a goal that they can identify and dream of. When they falter, remind them of their goal. Even if the goal changes, which it surely will as they learn more about different jobs and opportunities, the process is still important and relevant.

Children do some things well and some things they'd like to do better. Here is an exercise for building confidence.

Parts integration

Ask your child to hold out both hands turned upwards. In the one hand, ask them to imagine they have the thing they can do well. Let's say it's colouring. Ask them how they do colouring well. Maybe they answer that they concentrate hard, think about the lines they want to colour inside or they are visualizing how great the final result will be.

In the other hand, they should imagine they are holding the thing they find harder to do well, for example, writing. Ask them which aspects of the skills they use in the thing they do well could they transfer to the thing they want to do better. They have the resources; they may just need to apply a skill from one place in their work on another.

REVISION TIPS

Visual children should use sticky notes, mind maps, lists, read and make notes. This will help them visualize in the exam.

Auditory children should get a revision buddy to test them verbally. This will help recall what they said as they answered the questions.

Kinaesthetic children should use computer programs for bite-size revision. Interacting and testing themselves – the act of physically doing something – will help reinforce the facts they need.

Lots of parents feel anxious talking about their child's schoolwork to the teacher at parents' evening. Teachers get pretty anxious about this too! So what questions do you need to ask and how should you respond?

All the NLP guidelines on rapport are useful here because good communication is key, and you don't have very long to establish it in most parent–teacher meetings. Before you see the teacher, talk with your child about what they expect them to say. Ask them, 'If you were your teacher what would you say to us about you?' Use perceptual positioning where your child sits in a chair and pretends to be the teacher, then switches positions and responds as you, the parent, and then moves into a third chair to help disassociate and respond as themselves. This process allows you to be fully prepared for the teacher meeting and gives you time to decide in advance what questions will be most effective in the short time you will have.

Use towards rather than away-from questions, for example, 'How can we help Shana with her writing?' rather than 'How can we stop her mixing up her upper and lower case letters?' Also, aim for small-chunk questions in response to big-chunk comments. Teachers are inclined to start off big-chunk, for instance, 'I am very happy with Luca's progress this term.' This is not enough information. Respond with something small-chunk: 'Can you tell us in more detail exactly what progress you are happy with this term?' This will provide more useful feedback for you and your child. If your child's teacher uses generalizations such as 'Rebecca never concentrates in class', ask when she does concentrate. Does she really *never* concentrate in class or is it just before lunch when she is hungry, in certain classes or when she sits next to someone in particular?

Parents have a natural desire to know how their child performs compared to other children in the class. Teachers can be reluctant to give this information, so ask your child, *they* know!

Friends

Children often have a lack of confidence about making and keeping friends. Sometimes they imagine that other children are more popular than they are, that nobody likes them and that they have no friends.

This is usually not the case, but it can be their perception which is just as upsetting for them.

There are lots of practical things we can do to encourage friendships, such as joining them up to clubs and after-school activities, inviting friends home to play, taking a group of their friends out to the park or the cinema. However, the best thing we can do is help them find within themselves the confidence they need to enable them to attract friends themselves.

How do you do this? Teaching children about gaining rapport is a good way for them to attract friends. Basics like making eye contact are important, as is positive body language. Ask them what they notice about how 'popular' children behave. Pick someone they talk about a lot and ask them how you might notice them in the playground if you didn't know who they were. What is it about them that they notice? Do they smile a lot, laugh and look happy? What could your child do to be more like the popular child? Suggest they practise in the mirror or with a doll or teddy.

Popular children are not the ones with the most toys or the latest game cards, best mobile phone and so on. Like adults, popular children make connections with other children by their non-verbal skills and behaviour as well as their verbal skills. Suggest to your child that they could act 'as if' they are popular because this tends to translate into behaviour that will attract other children to them.

Here are some good ways to boost self-esteem, which communicates as positivity and attracts others.

Be nice
Open and positive people smile and make eye contact. Their smiles are wide and they smile with their eyes and mouth. They are friendly and make contact with others. The more people you talk to, the more possibilities that some will become good friends. Be generous and giving, listen actively and ask open questions rather than questions that just need a 'yes' or 'no' answer.

Children sometimes put up body barriers such as fiddling, folding arms and avoiding eye contact without realizing they do it.

Be yourself
You're not going to make friends with everyone. It is more likely friends will be people similar to you, so only by being yourself will

likely friends emerge. You don't have to change to be likeable; everyone has likeable qualities and people similar to you will recognize them.

Take care of yourself
Taking pride in your appearance and looking after yourself by brushing your teeth and keeping clean is all part of treating yourself as a likeable person. If you don't like yourself, then how can you expect others to like you? Another part of liking yourself is eating sensibly and exercising.

Make contact and socialize
The more opportunities you have to make friends by socializing, the more chance of making friends. You aren't going to make friends by staying at home. Teenagers often spend hours 'socializing' on Facebook or texting, but it's face to face contact and seeing the response from a friend to what you've said that builds friendships, along with *doing* things together.

Children sometimes show off in front of their friends because they want to get their attention. They don't think their friend will like them enough just as they are. Assure children that they are likeable by noticing and commenting on how likeable they are without showing off.

Keep it up!
Making and keeping friends takes time and attention. We need to give friends our time and care for them. If one of your children's friends is off sick or upset, ask your child what *they* would like if they felt bad, and help them make a card or phone call.

There is no failure, only feedback. This is an NLP belief and one that applies so much to friendship. Friends sometimes get cross with us and fall out from time to time. Instead of feeling upset or angry, think about what might have happened and ask them, because feedback is part of friendship. It may be that there had been a misunderstanding or one of you has said or done something hurtful and an apology needs to be made. *Give* feedback too, by saying when something has happened that you don't like; the friendship deepens and grows as you learn more about each other's needs.

Avoid making assumptions
Children and adults too often assume based on flimsy evidence. If your child says that someone doesn't like them at school, ask them

for the evidence and suggest they check it out. Children are much less held back than we are and will go up to another child and ask outright, 'Do you like me?'

A great exercise for building confidence in friendship situations is to use the circle of excellence exercise (pp. 95–6).

Tip

Confidence builds with positive experiences so just as it is easier to find a job when you have one than when you are unemployed, it is easier to find another friend when you already have one.

6

Guilty feelings

In this chapter you will learn:
- *why we feel guilt*
- *how to banish guilt from your personal life*
- *how to banish it from your parenting life*

We feel guilty when we think we have done something wrong or have, in fact, done something wrong. This could be 'wrong' in terms of the law or morality or it could be something that does not correspond to one of our *values*.

Guilt is an 'away from' emotion; negative and in its own way abusive if we carry guilt from the past with us into the future. Although we are not time-travellers like Doctor Who, and can't go back and put things right, we *can* time travel in NLP along a time line.

First, think about what your life would be like without this guilty feeling. You need to imagine letting it go and being without it because if you can't visualize that, it will be hard to let it go. Imagine how great it will feel to *not feel guilty*.

Guilt-free time travel

1 Imagine a time line stretching out in front of you on the floor, with the future in front of you and the past behind you.
2 Go to the point on the line where you experienced the situation or event that you feel guilty about.
3 Associate into it. That means really imagine you are there now, experiencing all that happened. You are the age you were when it was happening. This might mean you have to think yourself younger so picture yourself at that age wearing whatever you would have been wearing then. Picture the scene clearly.

4 When you're ready, imagine floating up above your time line and looking down on the scene you have painted. I want you to disassociate – see the scene as someone else would see it. You are the age you are now.
Do you see it differently now? Look for the positive intention you had at the time. What can you learn from the guilty event that you can bring into the future as a positive learning?

5 Let the emotions disappear as you disassociate and just look for the lessons and the understanding. You may find that at a conscious level you can extract the lessons, or it might be on a subconscious level that you take in the lessons and you just feel relieved of the guilt.

6 Now move back to the place on the line where you started and experience being *free of guilt*.

Not enough time with the children

Does anyone ever think they have enough time with the children? Well, yes, some probably do! It's extremely unlikely, however, that your children would agree. They want you all the time and they don't want to share you with their siblings. Therefore, this is potentially a real guilt-ridden issue because your time will never be enough for them. Given that this is the situation and that you will never satisfy their need for time with you, the only option is to make the most of what time you can give them. 'Quality time' is what it's usually called.

As children get older, their own lives get more interesting as they do activities after school and at weekends, and eventually they only want to be with their friends. Therefore, the time when they need you most is in fact quite a short period in terms of number of years, probably from birth to their teens.

If you can introduce your children to your own interests, you are in a win-win situation, achieving quality time for both of you. What can you do together that you both enjoy?

Insight

I love playing cards and as a family we have had many a fun evening and rainy days under canvas playing Whist and Rummy, Pelmanism and board games like Scrabble and Monopoly. We introduced our children to these

(Contd)

From an NLP perspective we need to reframe this common worry. First, we need to reframe it to a positive goal. Instead of 'not enough time with the kids', let's call it 'making the most of the time we have with our kids'. This is positive, but still rather vague. What is 'the most'?

It is in rethinking this goal and working out *what* we want from this time with our children that we establish the sort of parents we want to be. What sort of parent do you want to be?

We live in a hectic world with many demands on our time, but hasn't this always been so? It wasn't so very long ago when children were confined to the nursery and brought in to spend an hour a day with their parents before bedtime. We tend to think this unkind, but how many of us give our children an hour of undivided attention?

Insight

I find bedtime a very precious time when just my son and I are alone together. We can talk about the day, read a book and end the day on a loving and gentle note. This is even more important if the day has been stressful and there has been no quality time together. I take him up to bed early so this time isn't rushed.

Making the most of time with our children needs NLP rapport-building.

Match their program and language and you are well on the way to great communication. It seems very natural to get down to a child's level when we speak with them but we can also match their tone, volume, pace and rhythm of speech to connect even better. What we are aiming for in NLP rapport is to enter their territory and see the world as they see it so we don't waste valuable time in translation.

If your child uses this time with you to tell you about negative feelings they have of sadness or anger, again match their language and acknowledge their feelings, for example:

> *'Max made me really angry at school today, Daddy. He took my ruler and threw it on the floor, then the teacher told me off for dropping it.'*

> *'You were angry about that, I can see/hear/get that.'*

as opposed to trying to solve a problem,

> *'Next time, don't sit next to Max.'*

or advising him what to do,

> *'You should have explained what happened to the teacher.'*

or trying to distract him to make the angry feeling go away,

> *'Never mind, let's build something with your Lego.'*

We want to enjoy our children and as anyone with older children will tell us, the time passes very quickly before they prefer to be with their peers. Having fun together is key and you can do this by entering their world and finding the child in you.

Children not eating well

It's not unusual for children to go through phases where they use food as a battleground. It is a good choice because it hits us where it hurts most – as nurturing mother/food provider. It has maximum effect and emotional impact in a way that fussing over what they will wear doesn't. They will often combine this with a toilet issue, withholding it, refusing to use the toilet, wetting the bed and other high-impact strategies. We get totally frazzled, they get maximum attention, and this for them is success, albeit usually at a subconscious level. Of course it is not always as simple as this, as doctors will attest, but given that they all grow out of it and eat perfectly normally by the time they are adults, it must surely be a phase. Even as a phase, though, you need to take note and respond to their cry for attention. If you don't, it could indeed become a medical problem and that is a whole different ballgame.

Sadly, we are seeing an increase in serious eating disorders such as bulimia and anorexia nervosa. Although media do seem to be starting to take a more responsible attitude regarding their choice of models, the really attractive celebrities we see in the magazines and on TV are definitely not overweight! In fact, as soon as celebrities put on weight it is commented on; celebrity mums are praised for having returned to their bikini figure just weeks after the birth. How on earth are we supposed to match this?

But it's not just women – the 'fit' guys are slim, tall and have a 'six-pack'. We are now seeing boys getting a complex about their weight where it would previously have been shrugged off as girls' stuff.

The trouble is, children *are* getting fatter so we do have to show them the way, before we become a nation and a generation with heart problems. One of the difficulties is that with two parents working, or single parent households where mum works all day, it's difficult to find the time to cook what we used to call 'a hearty meal'. Jamie Oliver has tried valiantly to fight in his corner, but by the time children get to school age, the patterns have already been set. The time to address the eating issue is when your children are babies and toddlers.

As babies, we are watched all the time and babies pick up cues from adults about what to do, how to be with people, how to behave, how to eat and so on. If we don't eat with them, how are they to know how to eat? Perhaps we are aliens who don't need to eat? By far the best way to start your children eating well is to eat with them and for you all to eat one meal together that you can puree for baby, fork through or cut up, depending on your child's age. This way, children see the whole meal being eaten, including vegetables, so they know this is normal.

The trouble is that families come and go at different times and it can be hard to get everyone round the table at once. If this is the case with your family, try to get one person sitting down to eat with your youngest even if you just take a small portion and eat again later.

Insight

My teenage children tease me for wanting to chat with their friends at the table when they visit for dinner, but they all report back that their friends really enjoyed a family meal for a change!

TIPS TO MAKE MEAL-TIME FUN

Eating meals should be fun. Make it a chatty, lively time at the table, not in front of the TV where they are not concentrating on their meal.

▶ When you are trying to tempt your child to eat, think about their preferred communication style. If they are visual, choose different colours to make the meal look appetizing.

▶ Carrots are a great colour, peas and broccoli are fun shapes, and mashed potato you can make into any shape you like – use a cookie cutter and give them a car or a teddy bear shape!

- ▶ Use real meat, not processed meat. You could use a chicken breast cut into strips to make the frame for the meal or make it a star shape. Put it round the outside of the plate and count the pieces as they eat them.
- ▶ Fish comes in so many different types, so complement the colours with your vegetables; yellow of smoked haddock, white of cod, brown of tuna, etc.
- ▶ If your child is auditory, the sound of the food will appeal so choose things with different crunchy sounds or funny names that you can enjoy together. For a kinaesthetic child the feelings and physicality of the food will be important so they might enjoy fajitas or getting involved in the cooking itself, such as a stir fry.
- ▶ If you have older children who are learning to write and read, involve them in the whole process from deciding what to cook during the week, writing a shopping list, buying it and cooking it.

Insight

I pin our shopping list on the notice board along with any recipe cards I plan to use that week. The children are encouraged to add to it and stick up their own cards if they have a particular request. They love it when we go out and they can cook their own meal and now, as teenagers, have quite a repertoire of dishes they can make.

Children always eat better at someone else's house or when they have friends round. You are not running a restaurant so just make one dish for the children you've invited and they will eat it eventually if nothing else is offered. Go for favourites like spaghetti bolognese, macaroni cheese, home made pizza (fun for them to make and choose their own toppings) pasta bake, roast chicken or fish pie.

Insight

Visiting children to our house often start by saying they don't like something, almost as a default, but when they see everyone else eating it they make a brave start and without fail they finish it. I don't force anyone but then I don't offer alternatives. Giving the dishes funny names can also divert attention from what they 'think' they don't like.

If you are having problems with children eating, it is because they have discovered that this is a good way to get your attention. If they need your attention sit down with them while they eat, even if they refuse to eat it. Take an interest in them, their day, their friends, what they love doing. Avoid making meal time the battleground and food the weapon.

Children have all sorts of issues as they grow up and they need to be heard. Put yourself in their shoes – they want your attention, they haven't seen you all day. Of course they will kick up a fuss about food if it gets your attention. You can pre-empt this by giving them your attention as soon as they are home.

Coping with fear and anxiety

We all have fears and anxieties and, by now, well-established strategies for avoiding what causes them. With parenthood comes all sorts of new possibilities for fears that you hadn't discovered until you had children, so let's develop some new strategies that will not only help you rid yourself of the old fears but also these new ones. Children tend to pick up on our fears subliminally, so once you've learned how to do it for yourself, pass it on to your children.

Where do these fears come from? Yes, they do get passed down from your own parents quite often. It might be something said or done when you were young, such as a bad experience with a dog, getting stuck in a lift or a bumpy flight. It could be a result of unconscious habits, such as your mum or dad avoiding walking under ladders, taking the tube or flying.

Wherever they have come from, they are very real to you. There are two things to tell you, however, that may help with the process of getting rid of these fears. First, you were not *born* with them. Babies, when they are born, are not scared of flying, spiders, snakes or dogs. They quickly pick up our own fears and mimic them, but it is not inborn. Second, you picked up your fear in an instant and you can get rid of it just as quickly.

You have *chosen* to hold on to this fear, despite knowing that it is not logical. There are very few poisonous snakes or spiders in the world and they are rarely in your back garden. Most flights don't crash and most dogs don't bite you. It doesn't make sense to hold on to irrational fears, so unless you are getting any sort of pay-off for holding on to the fear, it is time to rid yourself of it. Most importantly, by letting your past behaviour limit your future possibilities you risk passing this limiting behaviour on to your children.

If your fear is more of a phobia, which is proving to be a problem in your everyday life, then think about seeing a hypnotherapist because this is a very effective way of curing phobias. If your fear is more of an inconvenience, then we can tackle it together.

Of course some fear is necessary, otherwise we would do crazy, dangerous things and hurt or even kill ourselves, so we need to weigh-up each potentially fearful situation and act accordingly rather than avoid it or ignore it.

Reducing fear

1 Think about the thing you fear most and picture a scene with you in it and experiencing the fear. It may be a fear you have actually experienced or it can be something you fear might happen. Really think about it deeply and blot everything else out. This is 'associating' into the experience as if you are going through it right now.
2 Rate the fear on a scale of one to ten.
3 Now imagine you are watching the same scene but you are watching it on a TV screen. Run the movie from before you felt uncomfortable, through to the bad experience, but when you do it add some funny effects as if you're producing a comedy sketch. Give yourself a funny hat or bizarre hairstyle and if it's an animal you're frightened of, give it a pair of sunglasses. Be creative and make it a bit of a Laurel and Hardy or Mr Bean type of movie. Give it a flavour of your favourite cartoon character or comedian.
4 Rewind the scene until you get back to *before* the fearful thing occurred and keep running the funny scene through as if you were watching a funny video clip again and again.
5 Now rate your feelings again on a scale of one to ten. You'll find it much lower than before.

Fear has a positive effect as well as a negative one. It can stop you in your tracks and focus you. If you suddenly see something frightening, you stop and take self-preservation action. For example, if a child is crossing a road and suddenly sees a car, they will run back to the kerb and keep themselves safe. If there was no fear, they might carry on walking. Fear can also energize you; you can run faster than you ever thought possible if you are afraid of something, like a bull in a field, for instance. We need to teach children to access their fears and sort them into unrealistic fears, such as monsters under the bed, which simply can't exist, and realistic fears that we can help them with by giving them strategies for coping.

You can use the exercise above with children for most fears as they are so good at playing imagination games. Another technique that will be helpful is anchoring.

Anchoring calm

1 Ask your child to think about a time when they were not frightened or anxious, maybe at a birthday party or playing with a good friend. Get them to picture the scene and really associate into it. That means they have to imagine they are there now and at the party.

2 Ask them to describe what they are playing, who is there, what food is there, what games, are there balloons? The more detail they can put into the picture, the better. Some children, especially visual learners and young children, will enjoy drawing a picture of the scene and colouring it in.

3 When the image is very strong, ask them to pull their ear lobe or do something that will remind them of the picture. As they do the action, they should conjure up the image until it becomes quite automatic.

They can use this anchor whenever they are in a fearful situation.

Sometimes children are anxious because of a limiting belief. They think they can't do something and are anxious about it, for example, taking part in a school play or standing up in class and speaking out loud. If these fears go unaddressed they can remain with a child beyond what might be called shyness and into the area of phobia as an adult.

Insight
I know adults who won't apply for a promotion because it would mean having to speak in meetings and network at conferences. They have a well-entrenched limiting belief that they can't do something because no one ever taught them strategies for overcoming their fear as children.

So how do you do it? Well, anchoring can work to some extent, but if a child has a limiting belief, this needs to be changed so it is no longer limiting. If a child believes that they 'can't', parents need to say 'But what if you could?' and invite the child to consider all the possibilities for them if they could overcome their anxieties. They must *want* to overcome them. At the moment they are getting some sort of pay-off for having this fear. This could be being considered sweet and shy, or being able to opt out of anything they don't want to do on the basis that they are shy. While it may seem cute to be a shy child, this may not be the identity you want for them as an adult.

Once they have taken on board what they *could* do if they were not shy, ask them to notice the behaviour of children they know who are not shy. How do they do it? How do you as an adult show 'not being shy', or are they modelling your own shyness?

Ask them to copy the children who are not shy. Perhaps they could spend more time with them and try to be more like them. Shy children often choose to play with other shy children because it's a safe strategy, but playing with bolder children gives them other possibilities that they might enjoy.

Insight

I once took my son to a leisure pool with slides and chutes, water cascades, a pirate ship and a wave machine. My son is not shy and he loved the frisson he got from the speed of the rapids and the slides. His friend spent the whole time clinging to his dad who seemed equally scared that some dreadful fate would befall him if he were to let go for an instant. The pay-off for this little boy was a long cuddle with his dad and not having to take any chances; he could stay perfectly safe and be rewarded for it. This might be fine for a boy aged five but how will he feel when he is invited to a party at a leisure pool when he is older – Will he have to decline the invitation? My son could have been a model for him but he was being *rewarded* for clinging to his dad. Notice where you put your attention – if you have a shy child, remember to reward the behaviour you want so they don't get rewarded for a limiting belief about themselves that will hinder them in the future.

Let them model being brave. If you need a model for other kinds of fearlessness, look among your family and friends. You can probably find someone who can model the skill you want your child to have. Your child will grow up with a 'can do' belief and reduce their fear and anxiety to what they need to cope with the occasional dangers in life, rather than imagining that there is danger lurking around every corner and in every situation.

7

....

Coping with change

In this chapter you will learn:
- *how to cope with changes in identity*
- *to help children adjust to big changes*
- *strategies to address fear and anxiety associated with change*
- *how to pass these skills on to your children*

Some of us like change more than others. It is natural to be cautious of change and want to cling to the familiar, but if these old patterns are not working we need to be open to changing them.

Change also happens *to* us. Through circumstances beyond our control we experience change and so do our children. This section works through some of the changes that might affect you as parents and offers some NLP-based suggestions on how to manage them.

Going back to work

This is a difficult question and one most mothers worry about. Should you go back to work? Should you take the opportunity to find other more child-friendly employment, assuming yours is not?

Hard though it may be, try to separate the whole financial side of the dilemma because, although that might seem hugely important, you may be surprised to learn that there are many lucrative forms of child-friendly work around nowadays, including franchise opportunities, work from home options and flexi-time work options.

Think about what you want from an *identity* point of view. Your identity may well have changed as a result of becoming a mother and whatever you had planned to do as your old identity may no longer fit who you are now. Employers are used to that, so find out what options are available with your current employer and how flexible they can be in accommodating your changed requirements.

So how do you address the identity question? Sometimes it can be helpful to use a time line for this. We have used it before in this book so you may already be familiar with the process.

Parts integration for change

Imagine a line out in front of you representing the future. You are standing at a point that marks today. Think about how you feel about your life today and what you would like to change about it. Think about what is working and what isn't working for you today.

Sometimes it helps if you mentally hold them in each hand; the things that are working in one hand and those that aren't in the other hand. This is called '**parts integration**'. Which hand weighs more? Is there anything in the 'working' hand that you could give to the other hand to help it work? Maybe you are managing to organize yourself really well at home but you can't seem to organize your childcare ready to return to work. Can you mentally hand over the organizing skills from home to where you need them?

Now move forward to a place in the future when you feel you will have sorted out the problem. Notice how far you have stepped; is it a long way or a short way?

How does it feel? What is different about your situation? What exactly has changed and how do you feel about it? Can you see more clearly now what you need to do to get there? What about your beliefs and values – do you have a clearer idea of what they are and who you are as a mother and as a woman?

Insight

My mother wanted me to have a well-trained, old-fashioned nanny for her first grandchild. She had a very precise visual image of a rather starchy, Victorian, uniformed nanny who would push her grandchild in a Silver Cross pram across Clapham Common getting plenty of fresh air. I, on the other hand, worked from home and wanted some flexibility to dip in and out of

(Contd)

childcare as work allowed, and the idea of some 'know it all' nanny being in charge (my perceptions only) didn't appeal at all. Instead I hired a lovely au pair from New Zealand who understood exactly what I wanted and was supremely flexible and accommodating, drifting in and out of her role effortlessly. My mother was horrified initially as Mags turned up for work on her first day to look after my precious one-week-old baby, wearing jeans and sporting a broken finger from martial arts training! But she soon grew to love Mags as much as we did over the three and a half years she was with us. Mags had no qualifications and relatively little experience but I loved her warmth and enthusiasm, 'can do' attitude and her sense of fun. Trust your intuition!

There is a lot of guilt around the idea of going back to work after having your baby and you may find the views of those around you quite difficult to manage because people can get emotional about the issue.

Remember that this is *your* life and *your* baby; trust your own intuition rather than peer-group or family pressure.

Childcare is usually the biggest consideration when you think about returning to work. If you're lucky enough to have your own mum or your partner available to look after the baby while you're at work, then this probably won't be an issue for you. If not, the choice may be between day nurseries, child-minders, au pairs or nannies. There are loads of books around offering advice about this issue and contacts for each option, so it won't be covered in this book.

The issue from an NLP point of view is more about establishing rapport with whoever is looking after your baby, knowing what you want from your chosen childcare option, communicating it clearly and being open to changing it as and when you feel something different is needed as your baby's needs change.

Think about how you phrase your needs. You may phrase them as big-chunk, for example, 'I just want my baby to be happy', but your childcare provider may need them to be small-chunk with quite precise instructions about what exactly that means on a day-to-day basis. You may think about what you *don't* want, away-from goals such as not leaving your baby unattended or not giving her processed baby food, but towards goals are generally easier to follow and are more positive.

You can use NLP modelling to help with the going back to work process. During your pregnancy and just after you've had your baby, talk to other mums about what they've done and how it's worked for them. Select a few models – mums who seem to have happily gone back to work. Ask them how they achieved this, what they felt, what they did and what 'was the difference that made the difference' for them. You will pick up a great many tips and useful bits of advice that may or may not resonate with you. It's particularly useful to tap into their belief system. What do they believe that made it a successful transition for them? Can you take on this belief for yourself and own it as part of you?

Trust that *you* know best what you want, then you'll *get* what you want. This will make going back to work much easier, rather than worrying about being away from your baby and whether or not you've done the right thing.

Not going back to work

Many mothers decide that they cannot go back to work after having their baby, either because the costs of childcare cannot justify it or because they simply want to be at home with their baby. This does not necessarily mean not earning because, depending on your qualification, there are many opportunities to earn money from home with reduced or minimal childcare. Here are just a few of them:

▶ Renting out a room or doing B&B on a small scale
▶ Running parties such as Pampered Chef, Tupperware, Body Shop, etc.
▶ Babysitting and child-minding
▶ Hairdressing, beauty therapy, reflexology, etc.
▶ Administration, database management, web research
▶ Writing, copywriting, press releases, proofreading
▶ Small business franchises such as molly maids, carpet cleaning, etc.
▶ Market research interviewing
▶ Dog-sitting/walking
▶ Tutoring/part-time teaching
▶ Fostering.

Check out websites such as mumsnet.com and workingmums.co.uk as well as a number of Facebook and Linked In groups that regularly discuss 'work from home' options and carry ads for businesses and work opportunities you can fit around your family with minimal childcare. Think about finding another parent to work with, so you can share resources and skills as well as the childcare.

There used to be huge pressure on mums to return to work and yet employers were reluctant to offer incentives such as part-time work, flexi-hours, working from home and so on. However, times are changing and, along with that, technology has advanced so much that many jobs can be done on a 'virtual' basis. It's certainly worth exploring this option if you don't want to go back to working in an office and be away from your baby all day. This then gives you more childcare options as you may not need the whole working day covered.

> ### Insight
> I run a B&B using the guest room as it's rarely occupied by our own guests. The government allows you to earn £4,250 per year free of tax on their 'rent a room' scheme, which means you can have a lodger or offer it on a B&B basis either to someone working in the area Monday to Friday or for weekend guests. It is fun meeting new people and takes up very little time if you offer continental breakfast.

Some women decide to set up a company because that would give them the opportunity to choose when and where they worked. They could then employ someone without children to take care of the office and enquiries so they could work largely from home and for fewer hours.

You don't have to work or earn at all of course, and if you're in the fortunate position of being able to afford this option then make the most of it and enjoy your time with your new baby. For many, this may be the first time in your life you are not working and it can seem very strange. Some find it more stressful because you can feel quite isolated at home with a baby all day with no adult company, controlled by the baby's needs rather than your own. To avoid feeling this you need to think about the solution you want, and make it happen.

Saying you 'don't want to work' is an away-from goal, so reframe it as a towards goal. What do you want instead? What would your ideal day or week look like? If you can't imagine it, how can you make it happen?

NLP talks about being solution-focused. This means thinking about solutions to the question of what you want from life for you and your baby.

> Find models for the life you want among your peers. Do you see a mum who you think seems to be living the life you want? Ask her how she does it and copy her strategy.

There are usually lots of local mother and baby activities you can join and you'll find details at your local library and in your local paper. There are also classes and activities that offer crèche facilities so you can go and do something on your own as well.

This is a great opportunity for you to do something new. Many local colleges run courses in the evening so perhaps you can go once your partner is home from work. You could learn a new skill or train for a career that is more family-friendly. Is there something you've always wanted to do? Teaching has always appealed to mums because of the term-time working, although hours are often longer than you think because of preparation time, meetings and marking. In some cases, grants are available to train as a teacher and many colleges have their own on-site crèche.

> The Open University has courses on just about everything and you can fit the work around your family, taking it a module at a time. You can be very flexible and complete an Open Degree, which means you can combine almost any modules you find interesting and accumulate points over the years. The courses have a variety of ways of studying and tutorials are usually held on a Saturday.

In your working life you may not have had time to cook, exercise, play a musical instrument or write, so although babies can be very time consuming, think about how you want to develop as a mother, and an individual, and what you'd like to do for yourself.

Some mums describe their brain as 'going to mush' just after they've had a baby. This is partly to do with the lack of sleep, but also it can be because if the brain isn't exercised it can get lazy. If you find this happening, find some good brain exercises to do such as crosswords or Sudoku, take the opportunity to read one of those classics you haven't read since you were at school or write some poetry. Playing a musical instrument can be a similar outlet and it's something you can enjoy with your child too. If you don't have room for a piano, try the guitar or keyboard (which has the additional benefit of headphones so you can practise while they are asleep!).

Not going back to work is a choice, a positive choice, and should be expressed as a towards goal, so don't tell people, 'I don't work'; tell them what you *do* do.

Becoming a stay-at-home dad

It is no longer unusual to see dads with children during the week. It used to just be weekends but now there are significant numbers of parents for whom the choice of who will stay at home and look after the children is not the traditional one. The recent global financial crisis has caused most of us to rethink what's important, and although we all have bills to pay, some parents are weighing up the costs of childcare against what they could earn and deciding that the best option from everyone's point of view is for Dad to be Mum. Hence a new breed of 'Mr Mums', as the media would have us call them, has been created.

This strikes at the identity level of the NLP logical levels and dads will be questioning who they are if they have stopped being the main breadwinner and have become the main childcarer. If this is your first child, you are in a special position because you can make the role your own with no template to follow, set out and established by your partner. No comparisons can be made and you are on pretty safe territory. If, however, this is your second or third child and your partner was stay-at-home or main carer previously, you may be struggling to make the role your own as you try to follow in your partner's footsteps.

The first thing to think about is your identity. Who are you? What are your strengths and skills? What are you good at? Although your skills may be inextricably linked to your work role, think again! You are probably really good at negotiating, managing, delegating and rapport with all sorts of people you have worked with – clients, customers, colleagues. These skills are very useful in childcare. Write a list of all the things you are good at.

I am good at:

Now apply them to your new role. How can these skills work for you in a different way? What are your values? What is important to you?

CASE STUDY

Matt cares for his three children and has done so for years. He felt strongly about not being the main breadwinner and has made it his role to renovate the house to add value to it, researches ways to save money on the bills and buys wisely to save money on food and clothes. He thinks of what he is saving the family as his earnings, including of course the expense of childcare itself. He would argue that the value he has added to their home is more than what he could have earned, even bearing in mind falling house prices.

Mums take their children to coffee mornings and toddler activity clubs, music groups and so on. Dads don't always want to do that, but they will do other things with their children that mums don't usually do such as long walks, playing football and cycling. There is no one way to be a main childcarer and children will respond to having the attention of a parent who loves them. Be the parent you want to be, rather than copying others.

Tip

There are now many groups of dads who have started clubs and activities for other dads so they can have the sort of conversations about football and things they enjoy rather than having to join in mums' conversations at the school gates or at toddler groups. They share ideas and join other dads and children for activities.

Men have always been criticized (often in jest) for not being able to multi-task and they worry that this makes it hard to be a stay-at-home dad, but do children want a multi-tasking parent or one who gives them undivided attention? Working mums complain that dads at home don't do the cleaning or all the tasks they used to do, but are they actually giving children more attention by being focused on one task at a time?

Self-esteem often suffers for dads not working because for years they have valued having status, money and a working life outside of the home. If you are externally referenced and benchmark yourself against others and what they think of you, this will be more of a problem. Instead, work on being internally referenced. Weigh up your self-esteem by how well *you* think you are doing and if you still feel a low sense of self-worth, remind yourself of the skills you are using every day.

You will be happier in your new role if you have a desired outcome. What do you want to achieve as a stay-at-home dad? Work towards this goal, with 'towards thinking' rather than 'away from' thinking. Positive thinking with an end goal in mind tends to make us feel happier as parents.

Sometimes there will be moments when you think 'I can't do this', to which the answer is 'But what if I could?' because you *can* do it. Put limiting beliefs about your ability aside. We all have times when we lack patience or feel despondent but you already have the resources you need. Remember when you did have the patience or sense of humour or whatever you feel is lacking. It may have been when you were working or at school or college or simply last week. When you remember having had that skill, capture it and use it now.

If there's a skill you really feel you never had then find someone who does and model it. This means finding someone who you think does this skill with excellence. Watch them and ask them how they do it. Ask them what beliefs they have about themselves that enable them to do it so well, then take on those beliefs for yourself.

Insight

My husband has the ability to throw paper planes up and down the hall for hours and seems to get pleasure out of it, as does my son. I watched him and copied him, but in no way could I match his excitement or interest in how far the paper plane had flown or what slight alterations in the fold needed to be made to increase its distance. It was only when I matched his belief that it mattered to get it further each time that I entered that realm of childhood play. Modelling children and being able to enter their territory is a skill that dads can give their children, especially little boys.

Stay-at-home dads are not 'Mr Mums' – they are dads. You can be the dad you want to be with your children and carry your own identity, values and skills into the role to make it your own.

And then there were two

It simply isn't true that having your second child is just a repeat of having your first, is it?

While the experience of childbirth is not new to you, the whole pregnancy process and the birth are completely new for your child.

It will be both exciting and scary for them to see your tummy get bigger as your pregnancy advances, but confusing as well. However much you involve your child it is still hard for a child to equate Mummy's bump with a tangible baby. Even less will they understand the difference it will make to them. And it will make a huge difference.

Tip
Many mums encourage their child to talk to the baby through their tummy and to look at books with pictures of how the baby is developing week by week.

Insight
When I told my two children that we were going to have another baby, my eldest announced that if it was a girl she was going to be called Jessica... and she is. She took on responsibility for naming her and caring for her before she was even born and though they are both now teenagers, she still watches out for her.

For some time, child number one has been the centre of attention around whom the whole family pivot, probably 24/7, and this is perfectly normal but quite impossible once child number two arrives. You won't be able to give your first child even 50 per cent of the attention you gave him before. Babies are enormously demanding day and night. You will be tired and emotionally drained so the activities you used to enjoy with your child will be curtailed, perhaps even stopped if you've had a difficult birth.

It is inevitable that some jealousy will occur, but it doesn't mean your child is actively jealous of the baby. They just want your attention and it seems to them that by prodding the baby or waking it up, this will result in them getting it. At this stage even negative attention is preferable to no attention.

Tip
Be inclusive so that your child is involved and feels that they are important. You can do this by saying things like, 'Let's keep as quiet as mice so baby will sleep, then we get a nice long time for our puzzle.' Using 'let's' and 'we' assures your child that you are still 'together', and baby is no more important than they are. Children need so much reassurance during these early months that your baby doesn't need; physically, they are already demanding your attention.

Although babies need lots of attention, you can involve your older child in activities around the baby and still have some one-on-one time with them but this is going to be at the expense of other things like housework. I have included a chapter on prioritizing and certainly you will need to constantly weigh up where your priorities lie. It will be easier to delegate baby care than toddler care because although your baby needs you, your older child will less willingly accept a substitute.

> **Tip**
> In advance of the birth, encourage friendships with children living close to you so that if you need a break after the birth, you can sell the idea of a sleepover or time with a friend more easily – they will think it is a treat rather than feeling cast aside.

There are lots of expectations of new mums, be they first or second-time mums and it can be difficult to ignore these mores, especially in our vulnerable post-baby weeks and months. Be aware of your environment and recognize its impact on your life choices but be prepared to make choices as to how you wish to be at the next stage.

Your child's environment is probably much smaller and more insular. It may be limited to your home. The impact of a new baby is therefore far greater for them and it would be true to say that for them, life will never be the same again.

Your behaviour is the choices you make as to how you want to live your life as a mum, now of two children. The choices won't be the same as they were when you only had one, so remember you are human.

Your older child's behaviour may change because of the change in environment. It is not unusual for them to experience bed-wetting, shyness and clinginess, tantrums and eating problems. While these do get your attention, your child may only be doing this at a subconscious level because he feels insecure, confused and threatened by the significant change in environment.

Think about your skills and capabilities, what you do best. This helps you channel energy by deciding how to prioritize, delegate and where to focus our attention. Be aware of what you do well and how you can use those talents. Did you manage people of differing abilities at work, for example? This will help.

> **Tip**
> Mums are excellent at multi-tasking and can easily cope with the needs of several children, but what children want is not to have to share you like that. If they can draw your attention only to them, they will do. A good way to keep them engaged and feeling involved is the same way you might handle a business meeting, by using eye contact and humour.

Your child, even as a toddler, has developed some great skills already and the most useful is to model you. They want your approval and want to be like you; they want to be in rapport with you. Work with this rather than against it as you do things together.

How you use your skills will tie in with your beliefs about yourself and ultimately with your identity. Beliefs change and it is very likely that the beliefs you held about being a mother have changed now you have had your second baby, especially compared to before you had your first! It's healthy to revisit your beliefs and just note down now what you believe about yourself.

Your child's beliefs have certainly changed. They may believe they are less loved, less important and less lovable. They used to believe they were the baby but clearly that's no longer true, so if being a baby gets your love, that's how they will behave because they believe babies are the loved ones. They are not going to change their new beliefs overnight, so this needs work and attention.

Your child's values will be constantly developing as they get older. The arrival of a sibling may challenge some of these as they compete for attention, but how you live out your values will guide them through this difficult time.

Tip
This is a good time for shared activities. Maybe there is something you used to do with your older child, such as puzzles or cooking. The baby can't join in this activity so this can be their special time with you. You can make this more special by getting a new puzzle or buying them a chef's hat, something that singles them out as important to you.

Your identity has changed as you are now a mother of two children but your child's identity has changed more fundamentally because they are now a sister or brother and oldest child. Being the oldest will influence the adult she will become. First-born children tend to be more ambitious, take responsibility seriously, work harder, are more successful and protective of others.

Your overall purpose in life may be changing now as your family expands and many mums think deeply about what they want from life at this time.

The arrival of your second child, or third or fourth, will bring with it a great many changes, and using the NLP logical levels as described on p. 25 will help guide you through them.

Moving house

Moving house is usually quoted as one of the most stressful changes you make in your life, partly because of the financial and logistical aspects but also the emotional upheaval of moving from a loved home to perhaps a new area, away from friends and family. It is also often accompanied by a change of job and school, which can add to the sense of upheaval.

While moving house is one of the most stressful changes of your life, it is not necessarily so for young children. This is because for adults the process is usually fraught with the practical issues that accompany the selling and buying of the biggest asset we have in our lives. While we adults worry about the financial aspects, children are more likely to pick up on the atmosphere and respond to that rather than the house move.

There are lots of things you can do to minimize the impact of a move for children.

▶ Have open days rather than random viewings that involve frantic tidying up, toys put away and children farmed out to friends.
▶ Pack away and store all those items that you won't need until you arrive at your new house, leaving your home looking larger and giving prospective buyers a clearer impression of how their furniture will fit in your house. You can use a garage or shed for this or one of the many storage facilities on offer. If you already have a removal firm in mind they will take boxes for you ahead of the final move. This way you can remove clothes you don't need in the next few months, and pictures from the walls so you can freshen up the paintwork and present a blank canvas.
▶ Make the de-cluttering process a family affair so that everyone feels involved. This starts the process of moving in a gradual way so children can adjust slowly to the idea of moving to a new home.
▶ If we want them to trust in our confidence about the future, keep children 'in the loop' at the earliest stage so there will be no surprises. You can use your knowledge of NLP to minimize the impact.
▶ Focus on the compelling vision, the positive aspects of the move. What will the move give you as a family? How can you reframe

this for the children so they see it in a positive light? Perhaps there will be a bigger garden, bigger bedrooms, a dedicated playroom, proximity to friends or grandparents, new school, park or somewhere fun to visit such as a zoo or theme park? Is there something they would really like to be able to do which will be possible in the new house?

▶ Ask them what they'd like in their new home and write a list, or if they are quite young you could make a collage board. Look at magazines for ideas and get the kids to cut out photos of houses, rooms and other ideas that appeal to them and stick them on a board. This involves them thinking in a positive way about the move and may trigger some discussions for you and your partner as well! You can include samples of wallpaper and paint, pictures of furniture and so on.

You can use NLP to help in discussions about the move. Think about how your child prefers to make decisions. What strategy do you see them using? Does she like choices or does she prefer a plan of action without choices? A child who enjoys choices will love to open the post and look at the properties you've been sent or help you look online. A child who doesn't like choices may prefer to write lists of things to pack, sell, recycle or store. They enjoy labelling things and getting on with the *process* of the move.

For example, if you're talking about your child's bedroom in the new house, perhaps they would like to choose the colour scheme, type of curtains and so on, or do they want to give you a list of what they want their new room to look like or have in it. Does your child want to make a quick decision and get on with what they're doing or deliberate between the options, weighing them up in turn? A child who likes choices will be motivated by this strategy and you can use it to distract them from worrying about the options they are not being given, for example:

> *'Jack, when we move to the new house, would you like blinds at your window or curtains? Here, let me show you in the magazine.'*

> *'I like the blinds best, I think.'*

> *'What about the colours, they have a wide range of colours, don't they? Which do you prefer?'*

'The red would go with my ManU posters but the blue would look like the sky for my model planes.'

'You could choose this neutral colour for the blinds and choose red or blue for the walls.'

And so the conversation continues with Jack feeling fully involved in the choices he could make for his new room but at no point is he given the choice about whether or not you will move because that isn't his choice to make, it's yours. If Jack can be involved with choices that are in his control this will distract him from the bigger choices he can't make.

Olivia does not like choices, they annoy her and she's too busy playing with her dolls to want to engage in these silly conversations. She is a busy bee with lots to do, friends to chat to and play with, dolls to dress and undress and hair to style. Her mother knows she's a bit worried about all the talk of the move but for her, a different approach works best. Olivia likes to control and organize but not make decisions or choices.

'Olivia, I need your help to sort out your room ready for the move. Please could you take these stickers and put one on each of the things you want to take?'

'Can't I just take everything?'

'Yes, but I'm sure you want to make some room for new things don't you? It's your birthday soon and there are some toys in your cupboard you haven't played with for ages.'

Bear in mind too that your partner will either be a choices or process person and this will affect how much they want to be involved in choosing or just viewing and listing advantages and disadvantages or organizing to finance the move itself and so on.

Another preference we have is for big- or small-chunk thinking. A big-chunk thinker will focus on the location or house in general, will see the possibilities and not notice the detail. A small-chunk thinker will notice the decor, furniture and running costs but not see the potential so clearly. If one of you is small-chunk and one big-chunk you can use this great combination to see the properties from different viewpoints so you have everything covered.

If your child is a big-chunk thinker, they could be overwhelmed with the enormity of the change in their life and will not be reassured by small-chunk information about having a larger bedroom or a big garden. Equally, a small-chunk thinking child may dwell on the detail such as the new school or moving from friends and not see the big picture, which may be about living somewhere safer or with work for their parents.

Some people are towards thinkers and others are away-from thinkers. A towards thinker will be thinking about what they will be looking forward to in the new house – the big kitchen or the quiet street – whereas others are thinking about what they will be moving away from – the noisy neighbours or the busy road. Tune into how your child is talking about it and echo their words rather than mismatch, in order to establish rapport and shared sentiments.

Tip

Children have little control over this huge decision and can feel like pawns on a chessboard moved around by adults. Although they cannot influence the decision to move, at least let them feel they are involved in all aspects of it as much as they want to be. Not every child will want to be involved, so trust your instincts.

You probably won't want to take your child to every house you view but they should see any you're seriously considering so they can have an input. It will depend on their age how important you feel their input is but for older children and teenagers this is essential to their settling in and feeling secure. After all, the move will be most traumatic for them as friendship groups will be well established in and out of school and this move may be the first major change in their life. They may be leaving a boyfriend or girlfriend and this will be traumatic for them, especially if they don't drive or aren't old enough to travel to see them on their own.

There's never an ideal time to move a school-age child and the timing may not be in your control anyway. Moving during the school holidays means they haven't had the opportunity to make friends to play with at their new school and don't have access to their old ones. You may have to spend the first few weeks of the move travelling back and forth or having your child stay with old friends until the start of the new school year. During the early months in a new home you will need to do lots of listening and reassuring as they stumble through the agonizing process of making new friends. Accept that this is a difficult time for them and although you know it will get easier, they don't.

Younger children just need to be regularly reassured and important toys kept with them throughout the move and not packed away. If they can be left with friends or family on the actual moving day this should make your day easier and you can have their room ready for their return.

Maintaining communication and rapport among family members throughout a stressful process, such as a move, is essential and will ensure the change happens as smoothly as possible. You have limited control over the other people involved in the move such as banks and building societies, estate agents, surveyors, solicitors and the vendors, but you do have control in your own home. Use it to keep everyone focused on the positive move, the desired outcome and compelling vision.

Changing schools

Whether your child is changing schools as a result of a move, a change in family circumstances, a natural progression to the next stage or because they or you were unhappy with the school they attended, the result is still an upheaval for your child.

Assuming you know of the change before your child, you have the opportunity to frame it so your child responds in a positive way. To do this you will certainly have to put yourself in their shoes because it is extremely unlikely that your child's criteria for what makes a great school will be the same as yours. Even if they weren't happy at their old school, it was familiar, and even negative familiar faces and situations can give a child a sense of security. If it was you who wasn't happy with the school, your child could feel resentful about making a change and react negatively either at the new school or at home or both.

> **Insight**
> When my son changed schools he was looking forward to cooked lunch, sport and real science lessons with experiments and a lab coat! He really enjoyed shopping for the sports equipment and couldn't wait to play the new sports he hadn't tried before. By focusing on that aspect, he hardly worried about the fact that he wouldn't know anyone there.

Putting yourself in your child's shoes means knowing what matters to them about their new school whatever that might be.

Researching the new school on the internet, in local papers, and among friends and neighbours can throw up interesting tidbits of information that can endorse your choice and familiarize your child with the new school.

It is easier to deal with natural change as children move from one school to the next mainly because the previous school prepares them; it talks about the change and they usually move on with a cohort of buddies. Schools are usually pretty good at preparing children as they move to their next school and talk about what to expect. Maybe your child already knows children who go there and this helps them to settle in. Often they have a day in the new school before they go there so the surroundings aren't too unfamiliar.

So how can NLP help you and your child adjust to this change? Remember you both have the resources already. What other changes have you experienced? Has your child had to face change in other areas of life? Do they have a younger sibling? Perhaps they had to adjust to that change. Have you moved house or faced the death of a pet? Invite your child to think about other changes and how they coped. They need confidence to embark on this new challenge and they can access this resource through experiences that were successfully navigated already. You can encourage this by reminding them how well they adjusted to these changes.

If your child is feeling overwhelmed and thinking big-chunk about the whole aspect of the new school, you can 'chunk down' to the detail and talk about the individual aspects of the new school so he can think about them in 'bite-size chunks' which may be easier to cope with. If he is feeling bogged down in all the detail – the uniform, new teachers, different buildings, bus to school, new class and so on – 'chunk up' to how exciting the change will be and what going to a new school will mean in terms of new opportunities in general.

If your child likes choices, then look at all the options with them – after-school clubs, subjects, routes to school, uniform options. If your child prefers process and doesn't like choices, you can make a plan or lists with them of what they need to get for the new school.

If your child is towards thinking, talk about what they have to look forward to and if they are away-from thinkers, talk about what they won't have anymore, maybe a teacher at their old school whom they didn't much like or the journey to school. There's bound to be something!

You can use metaphors to put a child at ease about change. Think about the change in their terms and find a suitable metaphor or better still ask them to find a metaphor themselves. Ask them, 'What is changing schools like for you?' Some children can express it best by drawing: ask them to draw a picture of themselves in their new school. Some can express it as an animal: what animal are they in their old school and what animal are they in their new school? How do they get to change into that new animal?

> **Tip**
>
> If your child needs help with finding a metaphor, you could suggest one and they will respond in a way that tells you what their metaphor is. They will say, 'No Mum, it's not like that, it's like this...'

> **Insight**
>
> I asked my daughter what it was like when she was the only child from her primary school going to the secondary school she chose. I knew how much she wanted to go, but imagined that she would be scared because that is how *I* would have felt. Her answer surprised me:
>
> 'A baby lion cub taking its first steps onto the African plains.'
>
> 'How is the baby lion feeling?' I asked.
>
> 'It was really scary, the baby cub wobbling onto the large African plains. My little wobbly legs stepping into the big wide world.'
>
> Knowing this was her feeling of 'scary', I was able to give her the support and encouragement she needed.

Another type of metaphor is the *story*. Can you tell your child a story about how you adjusted to the change of schools when you were young? Do you have a friend who has told you about their child changing schools and how they overcame their worries? Children love stories, especially about people they know. Here's an example of how this can work.

> *'Have I told you about George? He seems so grown up now, doesn't he, but did you know that he was so worried about going to his new school he used to wet the bed? He hid his*

new school uniform because he thought if he didn't have the uniform, he wouldn't be able to go. His mum tried everything to persuade him that he'd really enjoy the new school but nothing seemed to work. Then one day she watched him looking at some children getting off the bus and she realized he'd never been on a bus before on his own – could that be what it was? She was right. George was panicking that he'd miss his stop and get lost. So the next day they did the school journey together, there and back and talked about what to look out for so he knew which stop to get off on his way home. He was absolutely fine after that.'

This sort of story can trigger a response from your child about what could be worrying them and you can then address it. It's the not knowing, isn't it, which can be so difficult to work with?

Remember to tune in to whether your child is visual, auditory or kinaesthetic. If they are visual then they will want to look and focus on the uniform, the look of the buildings and see pictures of the school and the teachers. If they are auditory then hearing about it will work best and if they are kinaesthetic, visiting the school and being there for an open day will be important.

Going to a new school is an adventure and some children are braver than others, and have more self-confidence. You can build their confidence by reminding them of all the things they can do well, the resources they have and the skills they have. Avoid giving them limiting beliefs about themselves. Focus on what they can do and what they will be able to do. Get them to think about their desired outcome. What do they want to achieve at this new school and what are the steps along the way on that journey?

Divorce/separation/illness/death

There are some changes that we don't make by choice; they are imposed on us and we have to make adjustments quickly and from a sad place. What can make this even harder is the fact that we are responsible for our children who look to us for reassurance at a time when we may have none to give. Platitudes come naturally as we seek to set their minds at rest about the changing situation, but it can be hard to explain how things will be when maybe we don't even know ourselves.

All these changes are very hard to take on board for children because the family is the centre of their world so any major change like this will be very unsettling. Unable to express how upset and often angry they are about it, they can respond with non-verbal behaviour such as bedwetting and eating problems, withdrawal and other manifestations of hurt and overwhelm. This makes a difficult situation for us even worse as we have them to worry about as well as ourselves.

I know it is hard, but focus on a desired outcome by using a time line exercise with them.

Time line exercise for grief

1 Imagine a line representing time laid out on the floor in front of you. Stand at a point that represents today.

2 Discuss how you feel and listen to how your child feels. If they are visual, ask them what they see; if they are auditory, ask them what they hear; and if they are kinaesthetic, how they feel and what they want to do.

3 Recognize how terrible you feel now and acknowledge that it does feel bad today, rather than pretending all's well. This is about fully living in the moment. There could be tears and anger and this is OK.

4 When you both feel ready, decide on a point on the imaginary line when you think you will feel better than you feel today. This may be a different point for each of you and that is fine. Each of you go and stand on the point in time when you think you will feel less upset.

5 At that point (and notice how it is different for you and your child) talk about how you feel now, what has changed and what difference you are feeling in your emotions and experience. This may be a good opportunity for you both to share your thoughts about what needs to happen. Really associate into this moment in time and show your child how to anchor the moment so that at times when they feel bad, they can use the anchor to remind them that things will get better for them.

6 Now take a step back towards today's point, just as far as you feel comfortable, not necessarily all the way back. There may be a point along the way where you feel it marks a change.

> Talk about what that change could be and what you both
> want to happen.
> 7 Then go back to today's point on the line and talk about what
> you can do today to start to make the change.

Hopefully you will have found it helpful to experience the light at
the end of the tunnel and recognize that things will get better for you
and have discussed how that could come about.

Insight

When Grandpa died nearly two years ago, my children could not imagine
seeing Grandma on her own – without him. For them, the light at the end of
their tunnel was being able to visit without crying in front of her because they
didn't want to upset her further.

Some changes are just so terrible that it can be difficult to ever
imagine that there will be some resolution or that you or they will
be OK. You can use modelling to help here.

Is there someone you know who has been through something similar
to what you're experiencing now? Ask them about it and explore
how they managed to support their family and heal themselves. Those
who have been through painful times will understand how you are
feeling and will remember the poignant first steps along the road to
recovery. No one else's situation will be exactly the same as yours,
but by sharing the pain with others who can relate to what you're
going through, some models of excellence may be picked up that you
can apply to you and your family.

Here are several NLP tips that might also help:

▶ Use towards rather than away-from language with your children.
Rather than talk about what you no longer have, focus instead
on what you do have and joint goals you have discussed and
agreed.
▶ Get out photo albums and remind children of things they did
with the person they have lost. Remind them of the good times
and how much they were loved.
▶ Grief sometimes distorts images of the past and of the future.
Notice when you use words like 'never' and 'always', 'everyone',
'better' and so on. These generalizations and distortions can
be taken quite literally by children and aren't usually a fair
reflection of the situation.

- Use their preferred language – visual, auditory or kinaesthetic – to discuss their feelings.
- Step into their shoes to understand their territory. How they see their new world will be quite different from how you see it.
- As they steadily make progress towards coping with the changes, use anchors with them to remind themselves at less good times, that there have been some improvements.

However bad things may seem now, if you have a desired outcome that you agree with your children, and tie it down to specifics, you all have something to aim for. When you talk through with them what they think would be something to aim for, write down all suggestions and agree which ones will work. Then post it up somewhere so that everyone can see it and work towards it. Younger children may like to draw a picture of their desired outcome, so post that up as well.

We all want our children to have a happy childhood but sometimes it just isn't possible due to death, divorce, illness or separation. There are many books available on these themes and it helps for children to read them and know that they are not the only ones suffering. They also provide child models for them so they can learn from those who have been through a similar experience.

Death of a pet

The death of a pet, any pet, brings about a change in a family and is a huge loss for a child. The reason is that pets give unconditional love. Even mums and dads can withhold love when they are cross, and siblings certainly can! Pets don't, do they? Whatever mood you are in, whether you've done badly at school, fallen out with your best friend or shouted at your sister, your pet will love you just the way they always have done.

Children will miss its presence at every level and grieve for it. We too will grieve and in the process show our children how to do it. We are a model for them of how to cope with death not just of a pet, but any death. Sadly, pets do die and in most cases it will be your child's first encounter with death; one they will remember and learn from.

If you are reading this and you have a pet, think about how to prepare yourself for its death. This may help you decide what you might want to say to your child. Explain that animals don't live as long as we do and that one day it will die. To children, a week is ages so they won't be able to imagine ten years' time. Some people find it easier to explain it to children in terms of 'dog years' – that for every year of your child's age, their pet is seven times that. This will help them realize how much older their pet is than they are. It helps to know that their two-year-old dog is actually a teenager!

This also helps to explain how your animal ages from bouncy puppy or kitten to slower, sleepier and older animal. Comment on how much slower it is getting and how its hearing may not be as good as it was. You can prepare your child for what will happen one day without being morbid. This is an opportunity to teach them to be considerate and careful of their pet's changing needs.

Insight

Our dog Cocoa became old and our son Paul, at eight years of age, responded well to the idea that he needed to look after her now she was old. He must not tire her out and he should put away his Lego so she didn't stumble over it. As she neared the end, he made his favourite meal for her, scrambled egg, and made sure it was cooled before he gave it to her. He helped her up in the morning and went outside with her while she went to the toilet in case she fell over. The dynamics had changed and he was very sad, but he realized that he had an important role in the relationship. He said his goodbyes on the day she was put down and he stroked her and told her he loved her, but I felt that to watch her last moments would be too much for him. I knew from experience that dogs evacuate their bladder and bowels sometimes at the end and I thought he would find that too upsetting.

Of course, the death of a pet can prompt questions such as, 'When is grandma going to be put down because she can't walk very well now?' So, naturally, this is a good opportunity to talk about old age and quality of life.

It's hard to know when the right time is to have an animal put down and often we leave it too long and our pet suffers for longer than necessary because we are hoping against hope for a last minute recovery. Children need to understand that while their pet may just seem quiet, they may be in pain and it may be kinder for them to die now than wait until we are emotionally ready.

Tip

It's best to choose a time when your child is in a good state of mental health rather than just before an exam, starting a new school or some other stressful time, if you can.

There are different ideas about how to say goodbye to a dead pet. Much will depend on their age and how close they were to the pet. Trust your instinct to know how involved they should be in the final days.

Some people prefer to let the vet deal with everything and others like to be there until the last moment. Children are generally more robust than adults and honesty may be the best policy. If they don't see their pet dead, they may find it hard to come to terms with. Even children of a very young age like to kiss their pet goodbye and later in life if they haven't had this opportunity, regret it.

Tip

Put yourself in their shoes. How would you feel about coming back from school and finding your pet has gone? It's bewildering for a child.

Allow your child time to say goodbye and let them have time alone with their pet if they want to. The older a child is, the more important this might be. There are plenty of teenagers who can barely grunt at the rest of the family but are unstoppable in their own room with their dog or cat!

How you discuss the actual death will depend on how you and your partner feel about death and how you want to educate your child about it. If you come from a religious standpoint, then you may want to talk about your pet going to heaven or being with God. If you prefer to be more scientific, then you will explain how the body functions struggle to cope as the pet ages and will eventually pack up. Nothing really prepares us, however, for the death of a pet who is run over suddenly or who develops an illness and dies prematurely. It is going to be a shock for everyone and will need to be sensitively dealt with over time.

You may have decided to bury your pet in the garden, especially small pets like hamsters and fish. It helps the grieving process if you can involve your child in the burying by asking them to write a little poem or draw a picture to put in the grave. Mark the spot and say something nice about the pet to mark the occasion. You may want to plant a rose bush or flower on the spot as well.

Larger pets are usually taken care of by the vet and are sent off to a crematorium. Sometimes you can ask for the ashes to be sent back to you and you can bury them in the garden, again marking the spot with a tree or flower.

Why not help your child by making a small collection of photos of them with their pet and make a collage for their room or an album for them to keep for themselves to help them remember the relationship they had with their pet.

It can be tempting to dash out and replace a dead hamster or small animal or bird to spare your child the heartache of loss but this is not honest and children will usually notice, if not now, when they are older and wonder why their pet hamster lived for so long. Realizing that you kept replacing it might well lead them to wondering what else you were not honest about.

The grieving process is important for a child and cannot be shortened artificially by introducing even a really new pet. As they grieve, they are learning an important skill in life and a lesson that will serve them well in coping with the death of humans they are close to. Be there to support and comfort and let them comfort you as well. Talk about your lost pet and enjoy looking at photos and reminiscing about the good times you all had.

After the death of a large pet, the family change can be even greater. The loss of a dog may mean no more family walks and no dog to play with in the garden. Remember, though, it may also mean something positive. Without a dog you can be more spontaneous about going out or going away on holiday. Instead of dwelling on the negative side of being without your pet, reframe it as a positive; an opportunity to do something you couldn't do before.

8

....

Coping with conflict

In this chapter you will learn:
* *strategies for tackling bullying and sibling rivalry*
* *how to get your child to do what they're told*
* *to understand anger and jealousy*
* *how to cope with internal conflict*
* *how to pass these skills on to your child*

Conflict is, essentially, a lack of rapport. Although there are some personality types who enjoy conflict, the majority of us want to avoid it.

There are two types of conflict. *Inner conflict* is what we experience when our values are challenged, often by two equally compelling options. Then there are the everyday conflicts of sibling rivalry, pester power and jealousies that we have to sort out in order to maintain harmonious family relations.

Sibling rivalry

If there is ongoing rivalry, your siblings are not in rapport. Maybe this is unusual and could just be a phase, or perhaps the conflict falls more into the area of anger and jealousy, in which case you may need to read that specific section on p. 178.

By now you are very familiar with the VAK learning styles and can use them to help your children communicate. Suggest that they adapt what they have to say to the language of the other. By communicating in the same language they will not only understand what the other is saying or doing, but will better be able to find the positive intention.

Children frequently use distortions, deletions and generalizations: 'You *always* get your own way.' 'I'm *better* than you.' 'You *made* me cry.' Help them understand how to avoid potential conflict by 'cleaning up' their language. Words like 'always', 'never' and 'everyone' are imprecise and tend to provoke and inflame arguments because they simply can't be true. It is better to encourage them to describe what they have observed and clarify.

> *'You always get your own way.'*
becomes
> *'I notice that you got what you wanted.'*

> *'I'm better than you.'*
becomes
> *'I can read faster than you.'*

> *'You made me cry.'*
becomes
> *'I cried when you hit me because it hurt.'*

You can also apply PAC (Parent/Adult/Child) states. Avoid being the critical Parent and using words like 'should' when your children are in conflict because this can inflame the situation. Many parents wade into sibling rivalry attempting to calm the conflict, only to find both children jointly in conflict with the parent. Use the Adult mode, which is straightforward, reasonable communication expressing or requesting facts and information.

The chances are that your children are both in Child mode, feeling misunderstood, hurt and angry. In order to bring them into rapport with each other, you will need to draw out the Adult in them and build rapport using the VAK and meta programme knowledge you have now.

Demonstrate the Adult by asking direct questions to gather information which will be, in almost every case, more effective. Sibling rivalry is often escalated by an older child being in critical Parent mode and the younger child resenting it.

Here is an example of where Hannah (visual), the older sibling, is in critical Parent mode and then how it sounds (Ben is auditory) to the younger sibling.

Here, Hannah switches to a basic, honest request without judging or being critical.

| Hannah: | Ben, your mugs please? |
| Ben: | Here you go! Thanks. |

Older children often use the Parent mode because they mimic us as parents, so if we use the Adult mode with them, this is a better model for them to copy.

Similarly, younger children respond in Child mode because they see themselves as the 'child' in the family. This can happen even when they are grown up because they have been 'parented' by older siblings.

Teaching children that 'the map is not the territory' is also very useful when you have sibling rivalry. How a situation looks to the younger sibling is likely to be very different to the older sibling. Encourage them to stop, and put themselves in their sibling's shoes for a minute, in other words, mind the gap. How do we do this?

Stop and think whether there might be another way of looking at the situation. Can you reframe what is going on? If your children are very small, you might have to help them by playing a game.

Have a go

Suggest they are in a TV show and now the camera is going to roll backwards. What would the audience see? They could even act it out. 'And what happened just before that?' you could ask each time. Once you have been through the sequence backwards and used the audience as a reference point, they will probably see how the situation developed and how it could be remedied, as will you!

Lots of quarrels are caused by one child reacting too quickly before they really understand what has happened. Using this approach above helps them to disassociate or step back from the situation and view it as if they were someone else listening in or watching the argument. What would this other person, the audience, see and hear and feel?

An extension of this is perceptual positioning. Decide which child to work with, probably the older one.

Perceptual positioning for sibling rivalry

1 Get three chairs out and ask your child to sit on one of them. That is Position 1. This chair represents *them* and when they are sitting on it they speak as themselves.

2 Then pick another chair and put a teddy, or something like that, on it. This is Position 2 and represents their *sibling*. When they sit on this chair they speak as their sibling.

3 Position 3, the other chair, is someone else; someone who is observing them, but not you. It could be 'Mrs Smith' from down the road or a relative they don't know very well.

4 Your child sits at Position 1 and talks to Position 2 about their feelings, what they see, hear and feel about them. They can express their anger, resentment, hurt or anything else, and they can be open and honest because the sibling isn't there in person.

5 Then ask the child to go and sit at Position 2 and hold the teddy. They are now responding as the sibling. What do they now feel (as their sibling) having listened to what they had to say from Position 1? Here, your child is putting themselves in their sibling's shoes and imagining what they might feel, see and hear.

6 Ask your child to replace the teddy and go back to Position 1 to respond to their sibling's response.

7 They can switch back and forth until you feel everything that needs to be said has been said. Now ask your child to sit at Position 3 and comment on what they have heard as an outsider. What have they observed between the two siblings? Can they come up with any suggestions or solutions for the conflict?

This is a fairly standard conflict resolution technique that you can use with a child of almost any age.

Sibling rivalry can happen at any age, even between grown up siblings, and is normal, competitive pack behaviour, although it can be exasperating for us parents and upsetting for the children when it becomes relentless. Learning about techniques to help them keep it under control and to a minimum can make for a more harmonious home environment and help them deal with the situation when they become parents themselves.

Bullying

It can be very distressing to find out that your child has been bullying or has been bullied. It can take many forms, from the more overt and often sustained physical attacks, to the covert sniping and manipulating behind a child's back. This can happen at school, on the journey to and from school, and of course by text and social networking sites like Facebook. Schools have policies in place to address this issue, which does, despite assurances from schools, exist everywhere, sadly. In addition to the exercises here, there are excellent resources to help you online at childline.org.uk and bullyonline.org.

Children and young people have described bullying as:

▶ being called names
▶ being teased
▶ being pushed or pulled about
▶ having money and other possessions taken or messed about with
▶ having rumours spread about them
▶ being ignored and left out
▶ being hit, kicked or physically hurt in any way
▶ being threatened or intimidated.

If your child is being bullied in person or online, they tend to blame themselves but it is not their fault. They need to talk to you about it and you need to speak to your child's school. Children are reluctant, however, to admit that they are being bullied because they blame themselves and fear that if they tell the teacher, they will be bullied more, not less. If they retaliate, bullies can be very sneaky and can turn the tables by getting your child in trouble.

A good school will deal with bullying incidents quickly and firmly, but some schools ignore it and claim it doesn't exist because they fear bad publicity.

Encourage your child to think of an adult in the school they can talk to if they are being bullied – this may be a Teaching Assistant or dinner lady, and may not necessarily be their own teacher.

Children can be scarred for life as a result of bullying, so they need to respond promptly with names, instances and dates. Bullies want a response, that's why they are doing it. Telling your child to ignore it is to undermine their right to stand up for themselves and reinforces their belief that it was their fault in the first place. It is really important for you to assure your child that it is not their fault and that they have the right not to be hurt. NLP can help you with teaching your child how to defend themselves verbally, because not responding will result in the bullying continuing. Laughing at them may result in worse and fighting back can result in the victim being punished.

What we need to do as parents then is to arm our children with good self-esteem and mechanisms for achieving rapport through both verbal and non-verbal communication.

Acting skills can be really useful in bullying stand-offs. Your child needs to practise at home first and then act 'as if' when the bully approaches. To do this with the best effect, they need to anchor a confident feeling.

Anchoring confidence

Talk with your child about when they feel 'top dog' or full of confidence. Are they great on the sports field; are they great in the classroom? When your child gets an A or ten out of ten in a test, how do they feel? Do they sing well or are they great at playing a musical instrument? Whatever they do really well, ask them to focus on it and capture that feeling of achievement, great self-esteem and all-round power and control. When they have it, show them how to anchor it.

They will need to practise it a few times to really get it firmly established as an anchor, especially if they are going to have to use it in a vulnerable situation.

What they need to be able to do is apply their anchor as soon as they see the bully approach and get that instant confidence fix. This will change their body posture and general demeanour so that they give off a 'don't mess with me' message.

Children can practise phrases at home that could be used as extra ammunition once they are in that confident zone. They will be more effective from a strong position than one of weakness.

Get children to think in a way that is towards not away-from. When children are being bullied they tend to think about avoiding the bully rather than having a positive goal of making friends with other children so they have a number of children they can play with in the playground or on the way to and from school. Bullies tend to pick on children who spend a lot of time alone or in a pair, and are much less likely to bully a child who is with a group of friends. Teaching them rapport-building skills will help them build more friendships and make themselves less of a target to the bully.

There is a lot of bullying nowadays through text messaging and Facebook and this can be hard to monitor when you don't have access to what children are doing on the internet. Parental controls such as filtering software can be used and you could ensure the computer is in family space rather than in their bedroom. Most children will password protect their computer which makes it difficult to see what they are up to online. Given the lack of control you can have over what they are exposed to online the only way to protect them is by using NLP to instil some self-preservation skills.

So how do you do this?

First, they need an internal referencing system. Children are often caught up in an external referencing system whereby they are influenced by how others see them to the exclusion of any self-checking. They follow the strongest in their peer group and fear exclusion by being different. How the others judge them will be how they judge themselves. This makes them very easily swayed by those who they think matter. They will also tend to have low self-esteem because their esteem is at the mercy of others over whom they have no control.

From a very young age you can start to instil this internal referencing system by asking them what *they* think. For example, if they have spilt some paint on the carpet by accident it would be quite natural for you to ask them to clear it up or help you to do so. You would tell them to be more careful next time. To encourage them to be more self-referenced, you could ask them what happened and how they would sort it out.

When they come back from school saying, 'Melanie said my hair looks gross', you ask, 'And what do you think?' Give more value to their views and opinions so they learn that these matter and that everything needs to go through their own internal 'computer' to check it against what they believe and what they value. Consider using questions like:

> *'What is important to you?'*
> *'What do you think about what she said?'*
> *'Do you agree with that?'*
> *'How does that fit with your views?'*

If these questions are asked from an early age, they will build self-esteem and allow your child to acquire a mature checking facility for difficult situations so that if they are bullied they will question themselves, 'Is this fair? Is this right?' and answer 'No it isn't.' They will be better prepared to take action than a child used to accepting what others do and say as correct.

The second tool they need for bullying situations is 'mind the gap': instead of instantly responding or clicking the send button on Facebook or email, hitting someone in anger or responding aggressively, we need to teach our children to mind the gap. It is particularly important on the internet because they are making judgements with no visual contact and have to determine the meaning of the message from the tone and language alone.

Questions children need to ask of themselves when they get a text or email or message on Facebook are:

Who is this person?
Do they know them? How well do they know them? They need to disassociate. Would someone looking over their shoulder have a different view of the message if they read it? What other possible meaning could the message have from someone they don't know very well? If they don't know the person, it may be better to check it out with someone they trust like a close friend, teacher or parent. Make sure they know that it can be dangerous to respond to messages from people they don't know and that they should never arrange to meet anyone they don't know. If they don't believe you then make sure they see cuttings from the newspaper, internet sites and information on sites like Childline.

What do they mean by this message?
Your child should think about what could be meant by the message. They need to stop, mind the gap, and decide whether and how it is sensible to respond. Sometimes children send messages that they haven't really constructed very well, with limited language skills and careless typing and the message received may not be as the sender intended. They should read and reread the message. Perhaps a friend could look at it if they are not sure.

How should I respond?
If there is anything they are not sure about or if they think someone is being unkind, malicious, bullying or threatening, they need to check it out. A response asking for clarification such as 'What do you mean?' or 'Not sure what you mean by this' will hopefully get the sender to think about what they said and resend the message worded differently so the meaning is clearer.

Should I respond at all?
It may be safer to ignore messages that sound unkind. If, once your child has thought about it, they decide that the sender did not mean well or was bullying then they can block the sender and ignore the email. If the message was seen on Facebook as a conversation between other friends but about them, then this is harder as the sender of the spiteful message did not send it directly. It is hurtful to feel excluded from a conversation in which you can't defend yourself. However, if your child feels the message or words used are not reasonable and that (disassociating) other people would also think this then they should not respond.

The main point to make about bullying is that it is always wrong to bully another child and it should not be ignored. We need to equip children and teenagers to stand up for themselves by using internal referencing.

Disobedience

This may be a hard truth to accept, but if your children are not doing as they are told you need to change *your* behaviour, not theirs.

Remember the logical level pyramid on p. 25. In order to change your behaviour, you need to change your belief about yourself and the values you hold about you as a parent. Unless you feel it is important for your child to do as he is told, your lack of belief will subconsciously be communicated to your child, especially if you don't follow through. Threats, for example, rarely work because most parents would never do what they threaten and children know this. Bribes also tend to be short-lived and lead children to believe that they only need to do what they are told if they are given something.

Decide on your desired outcome. What sort of child do you want and what sort of parent do you want to be? What will your ground rules be? How will you and your partner put them into practice and where will be your emphasis? We know that consistency is the key to successful parenting and it is much easier to be consistent if you have agreed what matters to you as parents.

We need to use the Adult mode (PAC) and VAK learning styles in order to give clear instructions to children. For example, let's say your child is interrupting you when you are talking to another mum. Your responses will vary according to your child's preferred style:

▶ (Visual) 'I can see you want to say something but can you see I am talking to Tom's mum? So please watch and when you can see we have stopped talking, then you can say what you want to say.'
▶ (Auditory) 'Can you hear I am talking to Tom's mum? When you can't hear us talking any more then you can say what you want to say.'
▶ (Kinaesthetic) 'I can feel you want to take part in the conversation but I am involved with Tom's mum so please just hold on until we've finished.'

Children will be more likely to listen and follow instruction if they clearly understand what's expected of them.

When they have done as you've asked, you can praise them using the same language style:

▶ (Visual) 'I notice you have done as I asked, thank you.'
▶ (Auditory) 'I can listen to you now, thank you for waiting.'
▶ (Kinaesthetic) 'I feel happy that you have done as I asked, thank you.'

Children love to hear you praising them, especially to their other parent, and it builds a belief that they are a child who does as they're told if they hear you say, 'I was so proud of Leo today. I asked him to wait until we had finished talking and he was so patient and waited.'

Tone of voice is also very important when you want your child to listen to you. Try this.

Breathing exercise

1 Sing a note, in your natural speaking range, and put your hand where you think the sound is coming from. Is it from your throat, your chest or your diaphragm?
2 Now breathe in and as you breathe in let your stomach relax. This isn't easy because our natural reaction is to pull our stomach in as we breathe in.
3 Now breathe out by pulling your stomach in.
4 Practise this style of breathing until you can do it without your hand over your stomach.
5 When you are ready, sing a note again and observe how it is now coming from your stomach and is lower in pitch. That is the tone you need for discipline, not a squeaky one from your throat.

If you don't believe me experiment on your dog and note how the lower tone imposes control and the higher pitch just results in a strange look.

If you don't believe in your authority, then your children certainly won't; so use NLP to build this belief. Some parents have the limiting belief 'my children don't do anything I say'; sometimes they even laugh about it with other parents. This reinforces the belief and, if overheard by your children, reinforces it for them too. 'If you always do what you've always done, you will always get what you've always got.'

Valuing the role of disciplinarian (critical Parent) is as important as valuing your role of loving parent (nurturing Parent).

When you apply the critical Parent role, this tends to result in a Child response which would be to cry, answer back or do the opposite of what you are asking. The critical Parent is aggressive or passive/aggressive whereas the desired response tends to result from using the Adult position. The Adult position is one of stating facts and observing behaviour, asking questions and agreeing resolution. It sounds like this:

> *'I see that you want to talk when I am talking. I feel cross about this because I need to discuss something with Tom's mum. Please wait until we've finished our conversation unless it is very important.'*

By this approach you are stating what you see, explaining how you feel and suggesting a course of action.

As children get older and spend longer out of your control, it becomes more important that they follow the code of conduct you have established. They won't necessarily agree with your instructions, so you will need to discuss compromises that meet your requirements more flexibly. This allows them some chance to show they can be trusted.

Parents who parent assertively have self-confidence and NLP can help here. Remember, you have the resources! Where do you have the self-confidence resource? There will be some part of your life, and it may not be in your role as a parent, where you *do* have self-confidence. Examine that skill and transfer it to your parenting role.

Karys is self-confident as a dancer and fitness instructor, which she does during the day while Theo is at school, and at weekends when he is with his dad. After school though, she admits she has no control over him at all. His dad finds Theo very easy to be with and does as he's told. Karys thinks it could be because Theo doesn't live with his dad and so is a little shy of him and doesn't want to risk him losing his temper. Karys is very easy-going and never loses her temper, but worries that Theo will get into trouble when he's older if she can't get him to do what he's told when he's young. Karys is always tired after a day at work and doesn't want to discipline Theo; she wants their evenings to be relaxed and without constant resistance. Theo knows this and plays up because he gets more attention that way. He'd rather have her attention than sit watching TV while she texts or emails her friends and pupils. Theo's dad, on the other hand, keeps the weekend completely for Theo, plays football with him and they play together on the Wii.

I expect you can see that Theo is demanding Karys's attention by playing up for her and this behaviour has the desired effect as she spends most evenings telling him off. If they were to sit down and

(Contd)

discuss what they each want they would discover that if Karys were to give Theo some dedicated time after school, he would be much happier, as would she be because he would then be more amenable to occupying himself while she did her chores later.

Even young children are open to negotiating. Disobedience often results from boredom, frustration and confusion over what is expected. You need clear and firm communication based on towards goals rather than what you don't want and to come across as loving and assertive. This will lead to a more harmonious relationship.

Jealousy and anger

Jealousy and anger both tend to be symptoms of strong emotions, particularly a sense of lack of love from someone whose love is important to you, such as a family member or close friend.

There are two types of anger: overt and covert. Overt anger is when a child (or adult) expresses their anger in an obvious way by shouting, losing their temper or hitting someone or something. It can also be expressed by crying, in some cases, and temper tantrums with very young children. Overt anger can't be ignored and is usually easier to deal with because of that.

Covert anger is displayed by a child when they hold their anger *inside* them. It is then expressed by non-verbal behaviour such as stealing, lying, bullying, bed-wetting or other toilet-related behaviour, not eating or deliberate disobedience. Older children may express their anger by self-harming, antisocial behaviour, smoking and drinking and other behaviour that is usually hidden from parents. This makes it much harder to cope with because the behaviour can be cleverly masked and can become a pattern that they can't get out of without some expert help.

Children are usually angry, as opposed to just cross, when they are misunderstood and can't get your love and attention, which they need to feel good about themselves. It frequently happens at a time of change that they are having trouble coping with such as the birth of a new baby, a move of home or school, divorce or separation from a parent or a change in family circumstances.

Children need to be loved and given attention, and at times of stress and change in the family it can be hard to find time to spend with an older child who is less demanding physically, but who, on an emotional level, needs love and support that they find difficult to ask for. In desperation, and often subconsciously, they find a way of getting your attention, even if it is negative attention, by expressing their need as anger.

Tommy showed his anger at having to change schools by stealing from his mother's purse, and it was some time before she realized it was happening. He also stole at school and was then excluded for a day. He had all sorts of excuses and even tried to blame someone else. By the time she realized that he was stealing, Tommy was angry with her for not noticing his cry for help. They sought the help of a counsellor who helped them to discuss the underlying sadness about moving schools and leaving his friends.

Children, and teenagers particularly, express anger and jealousy when they can't control a situation that they are affected by. They often can't direct it at the people directly involved and direct it at their parents instead because we love them. It can be difficult to cope with this anger because, often, we too can't control the underlying situation. All we can do is mind the gap – pause, reflect and disassociate. By doing that, you may be able to understand the cause of the anger. Although you probably won't have the power to resolve it, you may be able to restore their self-confidence so they can work out for themselves what resources they need to resolve it for themselves.

There are numerous NLP techniques you can use with an angry child to help them understand what is going on in their head and find their own resolution. The aim is to prevent the behaviour from becoming a pattern.

Role-play

Children usually have a favourite TV character or video-game character that is their hero.

1 Ask them which character they'd like to be for a day. Let's say it is Hannah Montana, for example.
2 Ask, how would it feel to be Hannah Montana? What would it be like? How would things be different for you?

(Contd)

Remind them of an angry scene they experienced recently. Children have very short memories, so select one that was in the last few days, even if it was not as major as others, because that will be clearer in their mind.

4 Ask them:

▶ 'What happened just before you lost your temper? How were you feeling before, what were you doing, what were you thinking and what was said?'

▶ 'At the point at which you lost your temper, what did you feel, who said what and what did you do?'

▶ 'What did it feel like as you were shouting/hitting/crying?'

▶ 'What did it feel like afterwards? What was going on for you?'

▶ 'Now let's imagine you are Hannah Montana. What would you have done in the situation before you lost your temper?'

▶ 'Now, remembering that, how would you behave differently next time?

If you have a child who expresses anger covertly you can also use these exercises, but encourage and reward them when they do express their feelings and teach them by modelling controlled anger. You can say things like, 'I feel angry when [say what makes you angry]. In that situation do you know what I do? I have this great way of stopping myself getting annoyed. I anchor a good feeling of [say what your good feeling is]. I'll show you how to do it, shall I?'

Anger and jealousy are more serious than sibling rivalry because the child (or adult) feels they have no control over their emotions or the situation. Internal referencing will restore some measure of control and exercises such as perceptual positioning and anchoring will calm the anxiety.

Internal conflicts

It is not unusual to experience internal conflicts as we negotiate the minefield that is parenting these days. We bring to parenting our own experiences as a child, our observations of our peers' experiences, our own hopes and desires and then the reality of parenting our own children. Many of us have also experienced step-children or have been step-children ourselves and realized that there are many different ideas of how to be a parent.

Sometimes we ask others for advice and NLP philosophy supports the idea of modelling excellence, so finding good models for skills we want to acquire is a great starting point. When you feel confused and torn between different options, seek out mums and dads who have successfully managed the same situation and observe them, ask questions and copy their actions and decisions.

Insight

Recently my daughter was applying for university but felt unsure as to whether further education was really for her. I believed it was, based on her grades and intelligence, her ability to cope with pressure and her independence. I didn't want to push her though, so I was experiencing internal conflict – to hold back and leave it up to her or encourage her to apply. Through friends I managed to track down other mums who had also had this dilemma. I absorbed their feedback and experiences and tried some on with my daughter. The elegant solution turned out to be encouraging her to apply for a selection of courses, one-year foundation, two-year diploma, three-year degree and four-year with a year in industry. My models had advised that having options worked for their children and then, nearer the time and following visits and interviews at the colleges, their own preferred choice became apparent.

Do you enjoy having choices? If you do, then be aware that internal conflict may simply be how you manage information; your preferred way of operating. While most of the time this isn't a problem, if others need you to make a decision or you need to exert discipline quickly, then you will have to acquire the ability to be a process person at this time. You can model this by finding someone you have observed who seems to make decisions quickly because they don't consider choices – they process or plan from step A to step B in a straight line rather than meeting loads of T-junctions or roundabouts!

Alternatively you could disassociate: 'What would someone watching/listening/sensing me in this internal conflict decide to do?' This is a good solution for teenagers because they need to make decisions quickly and often in tricky situations where there is peer group pressure.

Another option is to act 'as if' you were someone who makes decisions quickly and easily without considering the choices for too long.

One of the problems with internal conflict, that you don't get with external conflict, is that you don't get a winner. If two parts of yourself are in conflict, whichever part of you wins, the other part of you loses. In NLP terms we would want to reframe this as a win-win by taking the lost option and making it seem unattractive and undesirable. Here is an example.

You had booked a weekend away, just you and your partner, and your toddler was going to stay with your mum. On the Friday, your mum phones to say she is very sorry but she has shingles and can't cope with your toddler. In fact she needs you to help her by getting some shopping and walking her dog. You need to cancel your weekend but you are torn between that and other options such as leaving your toddler with a friend or taking her with you. You disassociate and decide that you can't let your mum down, so you cancel your weekend away. Now you reframe the lost options. Another weekend will be much better anyway, maybe the weather will be warmer, you can claim back the cost on your holiday insurance so there's no financial loss, you will enjoy walking the dog with your toddler and the hotel would have been crowded anyway on Valentine's weekend, much better to go another time. Be creative – in no time you will have so successfully reframed the other options that you convince yourself this outcome is really the best one.

Use perceptual positioning to resolve internal conflict. This is great for situations when you cannot completely identify the specific areas that are in conflict; when you feel confused and overwhelmed because you feel you are not in harmony with yourself but don't know (or can't admit) why.

Perceptual positioning for internal conflict

1 Place a few chairs as a group facing each other and sit on one. This is the first position. Speak from this chair about one of the issues in conflict, the most prominent one.

2 When you've said all you can for the moment, go and sit on another chair and respond to what was said at the first position. This will be from a different perspective.

3 Now go to another chair and respond from that perspective.

4 Keep going until you've run through all the different angles of the problem. Then go back to the first position and comment on what you've heard. The options may seem easier to identify now and you should find it easier to reframe the options you do not ultimately choose.

A great follow-on exercise is 'conflict integration'. Most internal conflicts will be framed in terms of the logical levels of environment and beliefs and values. They will be conflicts about how to spend money, spend time, how to bring up your children and so on.

Chunk up – chunk down

Let's imagine an everyday internal conflict – your child says she doesn't want to eat vegetables but you know she needs them to be healthy and have a balanced diet.

The conflict is at the behavioural level at the moment. It is about what you will feed your child.

Now 'chunk it up', NLP style, and the internal conflict is about attitudes towards healthy eating which is now at the next level up, values and beliefs about how to feed your child.

Look for the good intention. You want your child to eat something they like and you want her to be healthy.

Now look for a behavioural choice that will satisfy this higher logical level. Perhaps you can look at recipes that will be both fun and healthy for her to eat.

Use NLP to chunk up the logical levels and then chunk down again to find a solution that satisfies both areas of the internal conflict.

Tip
Another way of approaching internal conflict is called parts integration. Here we separate out the areas of internal conflict and find ways to integrate them. This exercise is about finding compromises or a middle path.

Parts integration

Hold out your hands, palm up, as if you were holding the conflicting desires, one in each hand. In the one hand you have

(Contd)

NLP can be extremely helpful in providing tools to resolve internal conflict by reframing, chunking up and down the logical levels and parts integration. Remember to also use NLP modelling to find models of excellence who have resolved these internal conflicts and try out their solutions for yourself.

Pester power

Children ask for things all the time. Sometimes that is fine and we let them have what they want and other times we don't. As they don't know what the answer will be on each occasion, they, hopefully being the optimistic little people we want them to be, take a chance. To understand this better, step into their shoes.

There you are in town shopping for things they aren't too interested in when they'd much rather be playing with their friends or watching TV. Then you pass a toy shop. Well, for them, that's got to be more fun than the shops you want to go in. Of course they will think of something they want to buy or 'just look at'. Children don't usually have the power to go shopping by themselves until they are teens, and they can't buy online yet, so from their point of view this is a rare chance to spend their pocket money or get you to buy them something. If you put yourself in their shoes you will realize that it may not matter if what you buy them is inexpensive, just so long as they have *something*.

Lots of mums use this as a bribe and say 'If you're very good when we do my shopping I will let you buy something in the toy shop.' Children understand this sort of deal but unless you define 'good' or even 'very good' it is hard for a child to work out what they have to do to get the toy. The word 'good' needs to be much clearer to work in this context. Children do find walking around shops very boring, so with the best will in the world, they will mess about. The more precise you can be, the more chance the deal will work. Pinpoint something specific such as 'staying next to me' or 'holding your sister's hand' or 'staying on the pavement' so your child can remember a specific instruction. It will still need reinforcing with 'You're doing very well at… You will be able to buy a toy at the toy shop soon.' If you can interest your child in the other chores you have to do before getting to the toy shop, this helps.

Jules and David know that their son Jack finds writing very hard and he tries to write as little as possible. He also hates shopping. But he does like eating! Jack's teacher suggested that Jules get Jack to write the shopping list for her. Jules tried it. She and Jack checked the fridge and decided what they needed to buy and Jack wrote it down. Jules bought him a red clipboard so he felt very important checking the cupboards and telling Jules what they needed. He hardly noticed he was writing because the job he was doing was more fun than his dislike of writing.

What Jules had done was to reframe the task. Instead of it being a writing exercise, Jack was now doing a very important job for his mum. They decided not to worry if the spelling was not quite right but when they bought the item in the supermarket Jack could see how it was spelt and remembered for next time. Shopping became much easier and so did Jack's writing. Jules was then able to view the experience from Jack's point of view. He no longer pestered her in the shops because he was fully occupied finding the things he had written down on the list.

The word 'pester' is an adult word. Children just think they are asking for something. The reason they have to keep asking is because they are not given an answer. If we say 'I'll think about it' or 'Not now' or 'Stop pestering me', these are not answers. Children need straight 'yes' or 'no' answers. If they think your answer is unfair they may persist in asking, but if we explain in a way they can understand then they are more likely to stop asking.

We need to know how to say no.

Ben was desperate to get a new bike. He had outgrown his old one and kept pestering his parents to get him one for Christmas. His dad had just lost his job and they couldn't afford a new bike right now but instead of explaining this to Ben they just said, 'We'll see' because they were trying to avoid worrying him. Ben kept on and on and his mum got cross and shouted at him. Ben was confused and upset. Then he heard his parents talking in the kitchen about it and then he knew that they didn't have the money for a new bike. He went into the kitchen and said that he didn't want a new bike now after all, but they still didn't tell him they couldn't afford it. Instead they said, 'Of course we'll get you a new bike.' Ben was confused. He was ready to accept that he couldn't have one right now and he would have been happy with a new Wii game, which was a lot cheaper than a bike. So he kept on pestering because his parents didn't know how to just say no.

According to NLP, we need to keep in mind a desired outcome. We need to know what we want from any situation or exchange. This has to be quite specific and realistic. In the pestering situation, we have to decide what we are prepared to do and what we won't do. We then need to communicate this clearly in your child's preferred style (visual, auditory or kinaesthetic). In the case of Ben's bike, the options would be:

> *'Ben, I know you'd love to see this brand new bike under the Christmas tree but we can't see how we can afford it this year. We can look into getting one second-hand, or you can look in the toy shop and see if there's something else you'd like and we can see if we can get one later in the year for your birthday.' (Visual)*

> *'Ben, I heard you say you wanted a new bike but we can't afford it this year. Why don't we talk about what you'd like for Christmas instead. How do you like the sound of having it for your birthday?' (Auditory)*

> *'Ben, I know how excited you were about the idea of getting a new bike for Christmas but we can't afford it this year. We'd like to think about getting it for your birthday and find something else a bit cheaper for Christmas. How do you feel about that?' (Kinaesthetic)*

In this example, Mum and Dad had agreed that they would get Ben the bike but later in the year. The desired outcome for them was for him to accept this decision and have something cheaper for Christmas. They communicated this to him in his preferred style and the outcome would have been successful.

Pestering is an interesting concept because all children do it but they stop quite naturally as they get older and realize what is realistic. What we have to do is understand their point of view, decide our desired outcome and then make our communications clear and consistent. Children will always ask for things but it doesn't have to become pestering; that choice is ours.

9

Teenagers

In this chapter you will learn:
- *how teenagers can be streetwise*
- *how teenagers can be safe online and on their mobile phone*
- *how to pass these skills on to them*
- *about healthy sex for teenagers*
- *how to stay in rapport with your teenager*

Every chapter in this book is just as applicable to teenagers as it is to children but those of you with teenagers will find this chapter covers some more specific issues particular to teens.

Although it's best to start using NLP when your children are very young, you can still learn with your teenager. Teenagers can be wary of new ideas, especially ours! Nevertheless, that's no excuse for not having a go. It will be in their own interests to resolve conflicts and negotiate later curfews, more pocket money and so on. Assume they have the good intention to find a solution and that NLP could be the tool to use.

Communicating with your teenager

By now you will have a very good idea of whether your teenager is visual (processes information in images) auditory (sounds and speech work best) or kinaesthetic (physical and touchy-feely). Communicate with them choosing words and images to match their preferred language so you connect with them. When they are talking to you, translate what they say into your own language so you can understand them. Using clean language helps too. Reflect their own words back to them with an upward inflection at the end to encourage them to say more.

'School's rubbish.'
'School's rubbish?'

This may seem obvious, but many parents would respond with the statement 'Well, you still have to go,' or 'It can't be that bad.'

Teenagers use text messaging to communicate and many prefer this to phone calls to save their credit, so if you don't already text them, learn to do it now. Many have phones with email capability, so this is also an option if that works better for you.

Teenagers hate being shown up by embarrassing parents in front of their friends in or out of the home, but there are many ways of connecting with them and entering their territory to get a better understanding of their world.

The map is not the territory.

This is true for teens just as for children. Their world is different from ours and it is a lot more dangerous with potential for exposure to drugs, alcohol, sex and violence as well as exam and money pressures.

You can learn more about their world by matching them. Watch the TV programmes they watch, listen to their music and notice what they notice.

Music connects with us on all VAK levels and the words can have a hypnotic effect. If your teen is listening to violent negative lyrics all the time, it is bound to affect their behaviour, possibly even without them consciously listening to the words.

In his book *Connecting with your teen*, John Oda explains:

> *Most songs that make it…are what I call a VAK, meaning the lyrics have visual meaning…and auditory tone, tempo and tonality. Most…are also kinaesthetic, meaning they appeal to the physical nature of the child including their feelings and emotions. Using all three methods…music effectively builds a subconscious bond… Consequently if the music sends a negative message while children are in this state, they will have strong desires to mimic the attitudes and behaviours expressed in the music… So when music artists talk about killing, sex and violence in their songs, and then your teen sings along with the music with feeling – his or her emotions 'feed' the subconscious mind and*

*create a belief... Therefore if your teen feels what the artists says
is true or the musician's actions on the video look appealing and
it matches how they want to behave – the combined impact will
make their actions fit what the artist is modeling.*

John P. Oda, Connecting with Your Teen: The 7 Principles to Resolve
Teenage Behavioural Challenges, Booklocker.com, 2005

They are much more interested in celebrities than we are, so finding
out some little known fact about a celebrity they follow will show
that you are in their world. Study them and their friends in an
associated way as if you were one of them without judgement but
with the eyes and ears of another teenager. Yes, it means watching
programmes you wouldn't think of watching yourself but you will
get an amazing insight into their world, their language and priorities.

Humour is a great gift in families and has an important place with
teenagers. Not laughing *at* them, of course, but noticing what they
find funny and making them laugh. Metaphors can be very amusing
and powerful as a way of communicating with teenagers.

Tip

When you want to make a point, tell a (short) story or make up a poem or
funny anecdote rather than make a direct criticism. It tends to work better
and creates a less antagonistic atmosphere.

It is particularly effective to notice behaviour you want to encourage
and feed it back indirectly. This can be done by talking to a friend
within your teenager's earshot. For example:

> *'Do you know, Sara took the dog for a walk yesterday without
> being asked. That was so thoughtful.'*

Teenagers sometimes go through phases of finding physical contact
with parents slightly awkward as they come to terms with their own
sexuality and are developing their own sexual relationships. Even
formerly affectionate teenagers may need you to initiate hugs and
cuddles. They still need them just as they need your love and support
so be prepared to take the initiative. Use these embraces as anchors so
when the going is less than smooth, you can anchor these feelings to
remind yourself of your loving relationship with them.

Be aware of their 'state'. This is the word we use in NLP to describe
mood and state of mind. Just as we have better times of the day to be

approached about issues that need our attention, so do they. Think about how to calibrate their state and your own, and how to read it so you can choose the best moment to broach an awkward subject. For example, lots of parents find it difficult to mention revision for exams. The moment they get back from school is clearly not a good one! Check out resources on the internet such as Bitesize, revision books and TV programmes that could be relevant and leave them casually where they might be seen. In the case of internet resources, minimize them or save them as bookmarks that they will see. Again, you can use the indirect approach for effective encouragement such as mentioning to your partner (in your teenager's earshot) of how well he got on with his exam revision yesterday.

Revision is tough, boring and time-consuming but necessary. Teenagers find it difficult to project very far into the future and don't seem to relate exams to getting an interesting job and earning money. Instead of talking about exams as something they 'have to do', which will result in resentment, reframe it as a step along the way to a fun job. Talk about what they might like to do, how much money they want to earn or what sort of car they want to drive. Find out what will motivate them, what their desired outcome is, and work towards it rather than having an away-from attitude, such as, 'If you don't pass this exam you'll have to retake it.'

Insight

It may seem a bit trivial, but I found that food played a big part in my teenagers' lives. They seemed to be growing at an alarming rate and constantly needed feeding. I made a point especially during revision times of cooking big nourishing meals that encouraged them to be in for dinner and ensured they were well fed and in the best frame of mind to work. I also suggested they invite friends round for revision parties so they would work, then eat, then test each other. Cook their favourite meals so they feel supported and loved at this difficult time.

Teenagers can have surprisingly low self-esteem, despite their bravado and apparent confidence. They tend to hold limiting beliefs about their abilities and are usually externally referenced. This means that they often compare themselves with others they feel are cleverer than they and seem blind to their own prowess. You can use NLP to help them overcome this.

Limiting beliefs are beliefs teenagers hold about themselves that limit or restrict what they feel they can achieve. Examples would be

'I'm useless at maths; I'll never pass this exam so there's no point in trying.' Remind them of good marks they've had previously in maths, times when you've been impressed with their understanding of numbers or good things their teacher has said about their maths ability. If there is some truth in their statement and they're not just being melodramatic or despairing, ask them who among their friends is good at maths and suggest using them as a model in return for them helping their friend with another subject. Explain that a model in this context is someone who has a skill they need. Tell them how to learn from the model by asking them questions about how they do what they do well.

When teenagers are externally referenced they find it difficult to recognize their own abilities and make their own decisions. How often have we been told that 'No one has started revising yet' only to hear from other mums that indeed their child started revising weeks ago but it isn't cool to admit it to their peers. Encourage teenagers to decide for themselves what they need to do and when challenged ask, 'And what do *you* think?' Instead of criticizing, make observations based on your own personal feelings such as 'I notice you are not revising/doing your homework/tidying your room/still smoking. If that were me I would feel a bit worried – how do you feel about it?'

Instead of facing conflict head on, reframe it as feedback and an opportunity to discuss possible compromises. It's tempting, isn't it, when you see your teenager doing things you don't feel happy about, to feel threatened and angry. It's tempting to want to punish and withdraw your support, but this is the time they need you most. There are two options you have: soft love and tough love.

Soft love is the easy one involving unconditional love, giving your teenager praise, time with you and hugs – the nurturing Parent of PAC (see p. 7) Tough love is the critical Parent disciplining, correcting and criticizing and giving conditional love. Frequently, with teenagers, we find ourselves drawn into the latter against our will because we feel compelled to take action on account of their behaviour. However, just as a toddler throws a tantrum in the supermarket to get your attention, your teenager also wants your attention and poor behaviour is the teenage equivalent of the temper tantrum, but often on a larger, more dangerous canvas. They are too big now for us to scoop them into our arms and tell them we love them and make the shopping trip a bit more fun. What we can do though is look for the good intention in their behaviour and use the logical levels (see p. 25) to help us better understand them.

If their *behaviour* is what is annoying us, this is at the *environment* level of the logical levels. Consider it at the *beliefs and values* level. Look for the good intention: do they believe they should be more independent? Do they believe they are adults? Do they value having more freedom? Discuss with them what they want and their options for achieving this – perhaps it is by choosing different behaviours.

Use NLP principles when communicating, such as focusing on a desired outcome – what you want to achieve – and let them suggest how it can be done so they take ownership of the outcome as well. Focus on towards goals, the positive outcome, not the cessation of something – for example, not 'giving up smoking' but 'smoking half as many cigarettes a day'.

Teenagers can be fascinating as they stretch their boundaries and grow into adults but adulthood brings responsibilities that can be hard to apply in a world where they have limited power – financial, status and emotional. The step of giving them the power to apply their responsibility means taking risks and trusting them. The extent to which you can do this will depend on communication and rapport which you have already built up and can continue to build up using NLP techniques of matching and pacing, clean language with no distortions and generalizations and Adult–Adult communication, rather than Parent–Child.

Here are some basic ground rules for teenagers.

1 *WHO ARE THEY?*

Talk with your teenager about their values – what is important to them about who they are. Their beliefs will be constantly changing as they encounter new people and have new experiences but their values will be forming at their core. What are their values and what keeps them centred?

Be careful of making assumptions about their values such as 'I know you don't care what I think' or 'You think you know everything'. They *do* care and they *know* they don't know everything.

Discuss with them what they want to do, what sort of life they want for themselves, what sort of person they want to be and what is important to them about their future.

Get them to visualize what they will be doing in the future. Introduce them to the time line exercise you've been practising in this book or ask them just to imagine one and walk along it in their mind.

You could also use the circle of excellence.

Time line exercise

1 Ask them to draw an imaginary line on the floor and stand on it at a point that represents today.
2 Then ask them to pick a time in the future when they think they will be happy and feel good about themselves. Ask them to stand on that point on the line and notice how far away that is from the point they've come from.
3 Ask them to describe how it feels to have come this far, what they are doing, what sort of work it is and what's great about it. Get them to paint a picture for you of the life they are living. They may not know what it's called but there will be elements of it that they will describe in terms of what they want from a job, for example, nice people to work with, office or not, creative or not, with numbers or words and so on.
4 Then ask them to take a step on from there – where to next in the future? What does that hold? Where are they now in their life path?
5 Now ask them to walk back along the line towards the point that represents today. When they get to today's point, ask them to review how they feel about the future in this moment. What is the first step they will take towards it?

2 CONNECT WITH THEM

Most teenagers don't want to be around their parents, but there are usually one or two activities you can do together such as going to a football match, the movies, a pantomime, meals out and shopping trips. You just need opportunities for chatting without the possibility that it could get confrontational.

Insight

I find car journeys very helpful for teenage chat. Without the face-to-face element and an open road with plenty going on, it's quite easy to bring up sensitive topics because they can gaze out of the window and answer more honestly, perhaps, than they would do if you were sitting opposite.

> My older son is very private, but when I drive him anywhere, I find out what's going on for him. If I asked him at home over a cup of tea he would clam up and grunt back 'OK'. I would learn nothing!

Teenagers don't necessarily want you to join in all their activities, especially the ones they do with friends, but take an interest and give their activities value, whatever they are! Their map of the world is different from yours, even from your own teenage experiences, but it is important to them that you can connect with it in some way.

3 IT'S NOT ALL ABOUT MONEY!

Yes, this is our old friend 'quality time' again. This is not about handing out money but handing out *time* to your teen. Make physical contact with pats on the back, doing your daughter's hair or nails, hugs in private. Make them a cup of tea and share a chat over it.

Make yourself available by not always being busy or watching TV. It may be hard for them to initiate a conversation if they think you are busy, so look up and give them eye contact to show you're there for them if they want to talk.

Just a short time ago I read an article in one of the papers about a family, with teenagers, who didn't communicate. This all changed when the mum took in a puppy for training as a dog for the blind. Having a puppy brought out the inner child in her teenagers, they talked as a family much more, went out for walks together and even took it to the vet together.

Ask your teenager how they are, what they're up to at the weekend, who their best friend is at the moment, how school is going and what they are enjoying. Give them 100 per cent of your attention and make eye contact. Open-ended questions that won't get yes or no answers are best and use your child's preferred language pattern.

4 TELL THEM YOU LOVE THEM

Not 'You know I love you, don't you?' but 'I love you.' Teenagers need to hear this time and time again.

Teenagers, especially girls, say this to each other all the time in quite a casual way so if your words are to have impact, saying them face to face will be more meaningful to them. Don't expect them to tell you they love you in return. It's hard when teenagers move from loving their parents to sexual love and for a while the whole 'love thing' can be confusing. Reassure them that you love them and think they're great and one day they'll surprise you by telling you they love you as well.

5 BE POSITIVE

Think about what you are grateful for about your teenager and look for their good intention. They can seem like alien beings for some time but be curious about their territory rather than critical and remember what you were like as a teenager – you came through it and so will they!

Teaching children to be streetwise

The first thing to mention is that NLP teaches towards thinking rather than away-from which means we need to think about our children being safe on the streets rather than avoiding danger which is how we usually think of it. We also need to focus on our desired outcome in terms of what we want for our children and teenagers. Do we want them to be constantly wary of danger or have the confidence to cope with whatever comes their way? Think about what state, or frame of mind, you want your child to be in when they are out and about.

What we want is for them to be in a resourceful state where they are confident that they have the resources to manage every situation. See the section on bullying in Chapter 8 for more on this.

NLP philosophy is grounded in the belief that we all have the resources we need and the ability to model those we need more of. Modelling is taking an example of excellence in the skill we want to acquire, observing the desired behaviour and copying it. We can get closer to the skill by asking questions about the model's underlying beliefs and working these into our own view of the world.

Let's start with beliefs. If our teenagers believe that there is danger lurking around every corner they will venture out timid and fearful rather than resourceful. Question your teenagers about their beliefs and find out what state they are in when they go out. They will, to some extent, pick up their beliefs from you so be careful not to pass on your fears and concerns. We all have them and we worry about our teenagers, especially when we read or hear about the dangers on the streets such as knife crime, drugs and alcohol. It has always been dangerous for young people, even in rural areas, but we are probably more well-informed about it now through the media and the speed of today's information flow. We perceive the situation to be worse than it is because we view it with our own eyes. A gathering of hooded young people on the streets can look menacing to us, but is that the belief of our teenagers? Probably not. To them, they see a group of friends having fun.

Most teenagers know enough about their local environment and friends to be safe. It tends to be in unfamiliar surroundings where they may be caught out and need to be resourceful.

Josh went to a party at a village hall in a neighbouring town with his mates from school. After the party they left the hall and when his mates turned left towards the station to go home, Josh turned right by mistake because he was reading a text message and hadn't noticed which way they went. Straight away, he was set upon by some local boys who didn't want him in their territory. Luckily he was only a little bruised, but it goes to show that in unfamiliar surroundings, teenagers have to be especially vigilant.

CASE STUDY

Being resourceful in the context of the street is about being alert, calibrating state and being aware of changing state. Calibrating state is something you can teach teenagers.

Calibrating state

Whenever you get the opportunity, ask your teenager to tell you what state they are in, then ask them about other people you see around you. Are they relaxed, happy, confident, depressed and so on? Encourage them to read the body language of people they don't know. Remember, teenage body language is different and what we might perceive to be menacing may not seem at all that way to them.

The more aware they can be of how someone is feeling in the moment, the more prepared they will be when that state changes, perhaps as a result of alcohol or drug use. Constant calibration of their own state and that of those around them will enable them to manage situations and move on when it changes to something they are not comfortable with.

Being alert is a part of this – it means that they need to be aware of their surroundings, who is there, whether they know them, whether they can be seen and if someone knows where they are. They will naturally exude more confidence and be less attractive to the bully if they are with someone, walking in a well-lit street and walking purposefully. They do know this instinctively, of course, but sometimes situations arise when they find themselves in precisely the place they don't want to be and they need to know what to do. This is where being resourceful comes in.

Teenagers need to believe that they *are* resourceful in order to *be* resourceful and you can build this belief in them by noticing and commenting on when they display this trait. For example:

> *'That was very resourceful of you to transfer your homework to a memory stick in case it was wiped off the computer by mistake.'*

> *'That was resourceful of you to leave earlier for school when you noticed it was raining.'*

> *'That was resourceful of you to take a banana to school to eat before the match.'*

Encourage them to think for themselves rather than ask you what to do and feed it back with the message that they have the ability to be resourceful. For example:

> *'Mum, what should I do about my homework? I left it at Jamie's house but I have to hand it in today.'*

> *'I know you are very resourceful Tommy. What do you think your options are?'*

Being resourceful builds self-esteem and confidence which is great protection for the street.

Most teenagers know to avoid eye contact with people they don't know on the street, but if they do get into a conversation, building rapport is extremely useful. In a conflict or potential conflict on the street your teenager needs to be able to handle the situation with rapport. While I have been advocating matching pace, volume, tone and style to achieve rapport throughout the book, I would not recommend getting into a shouting match with a bully as this can escalate the encounter from antagonistic to violent.

Rapport is all about making a connection, so if your teenager can connect in some way, a potentially dangerous situation could be avoided. They might suggest, for example, that they know a mutual friend, or ask them which school they go to, or whether they have seen a white car just go by because that is their dad come to pick them up (a lie but it could put them off). These sorts of response might make the bully rethink their proposed attack.

Your teenager needs at their fingertips a selection of responses that they can practise on you or in the mirror. They need a confident body posture with full, but not aggressive, eye contact, a few stock responses that could fit any situation: 'Hey it's Jo, isn't it? I remember you from school' or 'Got to go, Dad's car is just round the corner' or 'Was that your phone?' and some self-defence moves for emergencies.

Teach your teenager to anchor a confident resourceful state by remembering a time when they were in control, calm and self-assured, ready with the right response and exuding power. They can then draw on this resource whenever they need it.

Sexual issues

It may seem to parents that children are being exposed earlier and earlier to sex education and sexual images in the media. Even programmes for young children sometimes include kissing and sexual innuendos nowadays, so how do we give our children the information they need to make choices that will protect them?

The most obvious way is to model the behaviour we want for our children. By showing rather than telling them what to do and what you feel is acceptable, they will have an established moral code well before they need it.

A significant number of children today do not live in a traditional family of married parents – instead, families are often 'blended' with parents who have had previous relationships. This means that children are growing up in an environment where they can see that relationships are not for life. They see celebrity relationships are often short-lived and these seem to take prominence over those that do last. How then do we encourage children to form lasting loving relationships within which they eventually have sex?

As a result of what we might term a promiscuous society, there is a huge risk of contracting sexually transmitted infections, some of which can be life-threatening. Thankfully, schools teach our children about them and tell them about safe sex and advocate the use of condoms. Luckily, there is no longer the social stigma attached to buying condoms which means the process is less embarrassing than it used to be! If you know or suspect your teenager is having sex, buy condoms at the supermarket and keep them in the bathroom or somewhere they will find them without having it known.

If your children have high self-esteem they will be less likely to be drawn into abusive relationships or treat sex casually, mistaking it for love. We can encourage our children to have high self-esteem by using the NLP techniques in this book, anchoring resourceful states and drawing on their skills so that they love and respect themselves.

Kaylie was very jealous of Phoebe because she had had a nice boyfriend, Dan, for four years who treated her really well and didn't cheat on her. Kaylie's boyfriend hit her when he was drunk and was sleeping around. When Phoebe and her boyfriend split up, Kaylie offered to comfort him and they were soon in bed together. She boasted about it to her friends and she was ostracized from the group altogether. Teenagers will tend to experiment sexually with more than one partner, but there are still rules and values they should be guided by.

Being internally referenced is also very important as it ensures teenagers will decide for themselves what fits with their values and identity rather than just following the crowd. To encourage teenagers to be aware of internally referencing and to think independently, remind them of their skills and their ability to make their own decisions.

They will naturally want to match with their peers, but you may want to encourage them to mismatch in some areas such as sexual activity. Are there other areas of their life where they show they can mismatch? Notice them and show them how they have the resource to mismatch.

Similarly, you may want them to have towards goals regarding relationships, towards healthy relationships. Help them set towards goals by asking them what sorts of boy or girl they like and want to date. Some teenagers are motivated by away-from goals like 'not wanting to have no boyfriend or girlfriend', so you may want to get them thinking about what sort of relationship they *do* want.

Rapport-building skills will enable them to build relationships that are founded on similar interests, values and beliefs rather than just on sexual attraction. You will be modelling this in your own relationship with your partner, hopefully. Teenagers learn how to be with the opposite sex by watching you and your partner. They often get embarrassed about sexual conversations with their parents or sexual conversations between their parents, so sometimes it helps for them to talk to other relatives such as uncles and aunts to whom they can talk as adults.

Remember PAC (Parent/Adult/Child) and answer questions posed in the Adult mode using Adult mode yourself rather than Parent mode, such as 'you should' type answers.

Most importantly, we need to remember that the map is not the territory; our teenagers' map of the world is different from ours, and what we see is not the same as what they see. Sometimes we might wish it were because with our experience we can see danger signs that they miss. When that happens, simply say what you observe rather than make assumptions.

Minding the gap is a useful NLP technique. Before plunging in with your thoughts on their behaviour, disassociate and pretend for a moment that you are not their parent, but are an impartial witness. What would that person see, how would they feel and what would they hear?

In blended families where you have much younger children and teenagers in the same home, it becomes even more important to consider how you are modelling sexual behaviour. While teenagers may be embarrassed by seeing their parents showing affection, younger children need the reassurance that their parents love each other.

In families, sexual issues tend to be sensitive ones and you and your partner need to talk about what you feel is acceptable and what is not acceptable behaviour, then make your position clear with your teenager. They need to feel valued and loved, but being totally liberated and having no boundaries is not an option until they are legally adults. It is also not very loving and can be quite scary for them. You can discuss areas of disagreement by listening to their views and agreeing compromises. Do this in rapport and you'll keep the channels of communication open, ensuring your teenager values themselves and feels loved by you both. They will be more likely to find a fulfilling relationship for themselves if you have modelled that for them in your parenting.

Glossary

anchoring Using a visual, auditory or kinaesthetic cue to trigger a positive resource.

away-from Goals or thoughts that have a negative orientation, avoiding rather than seeking (**towards**).

big-chunk Thinking in terms of the big picture rather than the details.

choices (person) Someone who prefers to have and consider options rather than follow **processes**.

clean language Language that is free of **deletions, distortions** and **generalizations** and reflects the word patterns and language of another person.

deletion Where important information has been deleted from your communication making it vague and unhelpful. Typical examples are when we praise or chastise our children in a way they cannot learn from.

distortion When you impose your own perceptions onto the communication and thereby impair rapport. There are three types of distortion: assumption, mind-reading and cause and effect.

embedded commands Subliminal instructions received with the opposite intention, for example, saying 'Don't think about pink elephants' ensures that you *do* think about them.

externally referenced Checking in with others for validation.

generalization Black and white thinking based on limited facts and experiences which restrict your options. It can be demonstrated by words such as 'always' and 'never'.

internally referenced Checking in with the self for validation, not other people.

limiting belief A belief held about ourselves and our capabilities, usually inherited from our childhood, that prevents us from achieving our full potential.

logical levels A set of factors that define who you are. They include environment, behaviour, skills, beliefs and values, identity and purpose.

matching Looking for similarities to help build rapport.

mind the gap Refers to the principle of disassociating before responding, also known as *bridge the gap*.

mismatching Looking for differences in order to avoid the same behaviour.

modelling Using an example of excellence to observe and mimic the same behaviour or quality.

parts integration Resolving inner conflict by looking for what one side, or part, can give to the other side to achieve harmony, also known as *conflict integration*.

perceptual positioning Putting yourself in the other person's shoes (second position), an impartial witness's shoes (third position) and revisiting your own feelings (first position).

processes (person) Someone who prefers to work to procedures and does not enjoy **choices**.

small-chunk Thinking in terms of details rather than the big picture.

towards Goals or thoughts that have a positive orientation, seeking rather than avoiding (**away-from**).

Taking it further

Bavister, S. and Vickers, A., *Teach Yourself NLP* (Hodder Education, 2008).

Beever, S., *Happy Kids Happy You: Using NLP to bring out the best in ourselves and the children we care for* (Crown House Publications, 2009).

Biddulph, S., *The Complete Secrets of Happy Children* (Harper Collins, 1998).

Churches, R. and Terry, R. *NLP for Teachers: How to be a Highly Effective Teacher* (Crown House Publishing, 2008).

Faber, A. and Mazlish, E., *How To Talk So Kids Will Listen & Listen So Kids Will Talk* (Simon & Schuster, 2002).

Freed, A. M., *T. A. for Teens (and Other Important People)* (Jalmar Press, 1976).

Knight, S., *NLP at Work: Neuro Linguistic Programming, The Difference That Makes a Difference in Business* (2nd edition) (Nicholas Brealey Publishing, 2009).

Oda, J. P., *Connecting with Your Teen: The 7 Principles to Resolve. Teenage Behavioral Challenges* (Booklocker.com, 2005).

Sargent, E., *Brilliant Parent: What the best parents know, do and say* (Pearson Education, 2009).

Satir, V., Gomori, M., and Gerber, J., *The Satir Model: Family Therapy and Beyond* (Science and Behavior Books, 1991).

Stallard, P., *Think Good Feel Good: A Cognitive Behaviour Therapy Workbook for Children and Young People* (John Wiley & Sons, 2002).

Weil, G. and Marden, D., *Raise Happy Children* (Hodder Education, 2010).

Index

accidents, *85*
activity groups, *145, 147*
Adult state, *8*, 114–15, *175*, 176–7
anchoring, 20–1, *38, 138, 171, 203*
anger, *178–80*
anxiety, *136–9*
'as if' (technique), *109, 116, 118, 127, 181*
asking for help, *66–7*
'association', *44–5*, 52–3, *78*
assumptions, *14*, 128–9
auditory learners, 40–2, *47, 60, 90*
    approaches for, *78*, 97–8, *109, 135*
    schoolwork, *121, 123, 124, 125*
'away from' (thinkers), 42–3, 48–9, *62, 64, 155, 158, 203*
'away from' goals, 33–4, *203*
    see also 'toward' goals

'bad behaviour', *73*
behaviour patterns, *4, 20, 25, 26*, 73–6, *106, 150*
    'bad behaviour', *73*
    disobedience, *174–8*
    modelling, *16–18*
    teenagers, *190, 192–3*
beliefs, *6, 18, 25, 26*, 27–30, *31, 32–3*
    children, *151, 193*, 196–7
    see also 'can-do' beliefs;
        limiting beliefs
big-chunk (thinkers), 43–4, 50–2, *61, 154–5, 203*
blended families, *199, 201*
body image, *133–4*
boundaries, *85–6*
BrainoBrain, *10*
'break state', *78, 88*
breathing exercise, *176*

bribes, *175*, 184–5
'bridge the gap', *83, 84, 116*
bullying, *65*, 170–4

calibrating state, *197*
'can do' beliefs, *139*
CBT, *9*
change, 70–6, 140–65
Child state, *8*
    see also Adult state; Parent state
childcare, *141–2, 143, 144*
childhood, *26–7, 28, 98–9*
children, *13*, 18–23, *83*
    behaviour, *17–18, 20, 73, 150*
    body image, *133–4*
    boundaries, *85–6*
    communication, *50–2*
    confidence, *117–20, 125, 127, 196–202*
    control issues, *89–90*
    eating, *133–6*
    embarrassment, *107–8*
    friends, *126–9*
    goals, *124–5*
    jealousy & anger, *178–80*
    moving house, *152–6*
    schoolwork, *120–6*
    siblings, *148–51, 166–70*
    skills, *22–3*
    supporting, *66–70, 131–3*
    trust in, *91–2*
choices (person), *43*, 49–50, *61–2, 80–1*, 153–4, *203*
chunks (thinking), *61, 157, 183*
    see also big-chunk (thinkers);
        small-chunk (thinkers)
circles of excellence, *95–6*
'clean language', 9–10, *67–8, 69, 203*
Cognitive Behavioural Therapy
    see CBT

communication, *18–19, 55–76, 90, 117*
   delegating, *89, 92*
   desired outcomes, *186*
   teenagers, *188–96*
   see also 'association'; criticism;
      'disassociation'; feedback;
      language patterns; 'mind the
      gap'; TA
compelling vision, *35–7, 152–3*
   see also goals; purpose
compromising, *59*
confidence, *95–129, 171*
   children, *117–20, 125, 127*
   see also self-confidence; self-esteem
conflict, *166–87*
conflict integration, *183*
consistency, *74*
contact, *190*
control issues, *89–90, 91, 92*
covert anger, *178, 179, 180*
criticism, *114–17*
cultural background, *26–7, 29*

dads, *146–8*
day-to-day life, *80–1*
death, *159–65*
delegating, *89–92*
deletions, *56, 64, 69, 203*
desired outcomes, *39–40, 59, 186–7*
desired responses, *56–8*
diaries, *9, 35*
diet & food, *75, 76, 133–6, 191*
'disassociation', *12, 44–5, 52–3, 88,*
   115, 181
disobedience, *174–8*
distortions, *55–6, 64, 69, 103,*
   119, 203
divorce, *159–61*

eating disorders, *133*
emails, *173–4*
embarrassment, *106–9*
embedded commands, *14, 69–70,*
   103, 203

emotions *see* feelings and emotions
empathizing *see* 'association'
environment, *25–7, 28, 70–1, 107, 150*
envy, *109–12*
Erickson, Milton, *6*
exercise, *75–6, 97*
'externally referenced', *54, 103, 118,*
   172, 192, 203
eye contact, *58, 127, 198*

Facebook, *128, 170, 173–4*
failure, *11, 96–103*
families, *199, 201–2*
fear, *136–9*
feedback, *11, 96, 98–103, 106,*
   116–17, 128, 192
'Feeler', *9*
feelings and emotions, *57, 59, 73, 92*
   see also anger; envy; failure; fear;
      guilt; jealousy
food *see* diet & food
friends, *126–9*

generalizations, *56, 64, 69, 119, 203*
Gestalt Theory, *5, 6*
goals, *34–5, 39, 81, 124–5, 200–1*
   see also 'away from' goals;
      compelling vision; 'towards'
      goals
good intentions, *11, 12, **13**, 91*
'good mother', *29–30, 103–6*
grief, *160–1, 165*
guilt, *84–6, 130–9*

'having it all', *104*

identity, *24–54, 140–1, 146–7, 151*
illness, *159–61*
internal conflicts, *166, 180–4*
'internally referenced', *6, 54, 103,*
   115–16, 118, 172–3, 200, 204
internet, *172*
   see also emails; Facebook
'Intuitor', *9*

jealousy, *149*, **178–80**
Jungian philosophy, *8–9*

kinaesthetic learners, *40–2*, **47**, *90*
    approaches for, *60*, *78*, *98*, *109*,
      135
    schoolwork, *121*, *123–4*, *125*
Knight, Sue, *10*

labels, *65*
language patterns, *7*, *11*, **14**, *56*,
    57, *176*
    see also 'clean language';
      metaphors
limiting beliefs, *38–9*, *98–9*, *138–9*,
    191–2, *204*
literacy, *122–4*
'living in the moment', *53–4*, *77–8*
logical levels (NLP), *25–30*, *204*

'map is not the territory', *13*, *18*,
    168, *189*
'maps of the world', *6*, *9*, *45*, *201*
'matching', *53*, *58*, *59*, **63**, *132–3*, *204*
'me time', *86–8*
meal-times, *134–5*
measuring success, *35*
meta programmes, *40*, *54*
    see also; auditory learners; 'away
      from' goals; big-chunk thinkers;
      kinaesthetic learners; 'matching';
      'mismatching'; small-chunk
      thinkers; 'toward' goals; visual
      learners
metaphors, *19*, *22–3*, *158–9*
'mind the gap', *8–9*, **11–12**, *173*,
    201, *204*
mirroring, *58*
'mismatching', *53*, *204*
mistakes, *92*
modelling excellence, *5*, *15–18*, *81*,
    106, *108*, *110*, *142–3*, *148*, *181*, *204*
    for children, *67*, *118–20*, *161*,
      199, *201*

Montessori learning, *46*, *90*
moving house, *152–6*
music, *189–90*

negotiating skills, *59*, **63–6**
Neuro Linguistic Programming
  see NLP
NLP, *3*, *4*, *5–23*, *25–30*
NLP at Work (Brealey Publishing
  2009), *10*
'No', *83–4*, *185–6*
non-verbal language, *56*
    see also eye contact; 'matching';
      mirroring; reflecting back
numeracy, *124*

older children, *83*
'outcome thinking', *104–5*
overt anger, *178*

PAC state (Parent, Adult, Child), *7–8*,
    167–8, *175*
Parent state, *7–8*
parents' evenings, *126*
'parts integration', *141*, *183–4*, *204*
perceptual positioning, *66*, *111*, *126*,
    169, *182–3*, *204*
Perls, Franz, *5–6*
pester power, *184–7*
pets, *162–5*
physical state, *97–8*
positive goals, *48*
positive statements, *36*, *37*
praise, *22*, **175–6**
prioritizing, *82–4*, *149–50*
proactive responses, *62–3*
'problem thinking', *104–5*
processes (person), *43*, *49–50*, *64*,
    80–1, *153–4*, *204*
'programming', *6*, *7*
purpose, *25*, *26*, **31**
    see also compelling vision

'quality time', *85*, **131–3**, *195*

rapport-building, *6, 21–2, 56, 58–64,*
126, 132–3, 142
    children, *127–9, 172*
    teenagers, *199, 201*
reactive responses, *62–3*
reflecting back, *59*
revision, *125, 191*
risk-taking, *48*
role-play, *179–80*
roles, parental, *25*

'sandwich feedback', *117*
sarcasm, *11, 65*
Satir, Virginia, *5, 6, 60*
schools, *10, 126, 155,* **156–9**
schoolwork, *120–6, 191*
second children, *148–51*
self-confidence, *177*
self-esteem, *88, 110–11, 147–8,*
191, 200
separation, *159–61*
sexual issues, *199–202*
shared activities, *131–2, 151, 194–5*
    activity groups, *145, 147*
sibling rivalry, *166–70*
skills, *3–4, 12, 25, 26, 30–3, 100–3*
    new skills, *145*
    recognizing, *22–3*
    see also negotiating skills
small-chunk (thinkers), *43–4, 50–2,*
61, 126, 142, 154–5, 204
social networking sites *see* Facebook
socializing, *128*
solution focused, *14–15*
'state' (mind), *190–1*
stay-at-home dads, *146–8*
staying at home, *144–8*
streetwise, being, *196–202*

strengths, *112–14*
sugar highs, *75*
support strategies, *66–70*
swishing exercise, *115–16*

TA, *7–8*
teenagers, *179,* **188–202**
texting, *128, 170, 173–4, 189*
'Thinker', *8–9*
threats, *65, 175*
time lines, *37–8, 78–9, 87, 105, 160, 194*
time management, *77–92*
'towards' goals, *48–9, 193, 204*
'towards' questions, *126*
'towards' thinkers, *42–3, 62, 155, 204*
    approaches for, *64, 158*
Transactional Analysis *see* TA
trust, *89, 90, 92*
'trying', *12–13, 34*
TV programmes, *19, 189, 190*

VAK learning styles, *166–7, 175*
    see also Auditory Learners;
      Kinaesthetic Learners;
      Visual Learners
values, *6, 25, 26, 27–30, 33, 106*
    children, *151*
    teenagers, *193–4*
    time for yourself, *79–80, 81, 86–8*
visual learners, *40–2,* **46**
    approaches for, *59, 90, 97–8, 109*
    schoolwork, *120–1, 122–3,*
124, 125
    time lines, *78*
visualization exercise, *110*

work/life balance, *86, 140–6*
working from home, *143–6*

Image credits